The

Senior
Organizer

The

Senior Organizer

*"It's one-stop shopping for
all your vital information.
No more digging through files!"*

Debby S. Bitticks
Lynn Benson
Dorothy K. Breininger

Health Communications, Inc.
Deerfield Beach, Florida

www.hcibooks.com
www.biobinders.com

**Library of Congress Cataloging-in-Publication Data
is available from the Library of Congress.**

The purpose of this book is to inspire. The information is provided with the understanding that the authors, publisher and their related companies, directors, employees, partners and agents are not engaged in rendering medical, legal, accounting, tax, or other professional advice and services. As such, The Senior Organizer should not be used as a substitute for consultation with professional, medical, accounting, tax, legal or other competent advisers.

©2006 Debby S. Bitticks, Lynn Benson, Dorothy K. Breininger
ISBN 0-7573-0489-3

HCI, its Logos and Marks are trademarks of Health Communications, Inc.

Publisher: Health Communications, Inc.
      3201 S.W. 15th Street
      Deerfield Beach, FL 33442-8190

Cover and inside design by Karen Ross
Inside book formatting by Dawn Von Strolley Grove

Dedication

We want to thank our parents and grandparents for the privilege of caring for them and for the inspiration to create *The Senior Organizer*.

Keeping our loved ones organized and safe gave us peace of mind and more time to spend loving them.

Debby Bitticks
Lynn Benson
Dorothy Breininger

Contents

In Case of Emergency
Quick Reference

Foreword

When I first saw *The Senior Organizer,* I was thoroughly impressed. Here was the perfect book to help families and caregivers with an elder. It accommodates every need, from scheduling medical appointments and tracking medications, through recording key personal information to covering legal and financial needs.

I thought back to when we started caring for my mother at age eighty-five, and the difficulties we had encountered in gathering and organizing the most basic and critical information for her care. Then I thought about my father-in-law who had been diagnosed with dementia/Alzheimer's, and the enormous responsibility we had assumed in caring for him when he moved in with us. Finally my mind turned to my father, who had gone into a depression after his wife had passed on, and all the difficulties we had to deal with in arranging for his care, and his safety and well-being when he lived alone away from any family members. And now the book had been created that could save countless hours of effort and many lost dollars in trying to figure out what needed to be done and what information was necessary to help handle the medical, legal and financial issues that arise in these circumstances.

It is wise to complete *The Senior Organizer* while you're healthy and strong so you can get peace of mind, knowing that you're organized and equipped to handle all situations. No one knows when illness or an accident will occur, and the best way to be organized is to use this book to assemble all the crucial information in one easy-to-update location so it is always at hand.

I truly believe that this is the perfect book at the right time to help millions of people, whether organizing yourself or helping a loved one who is aging and needing more care. Your ability to focus on caring rather than being forced to frantically try to locate important documents during a time of crisis will be deeply appreciated. Using this book will soon become second nature, and the initial effort of gathering the needed documents and information will be amply rewarded each time there is a doctor's appointment, or a trip to the hospital, the CPA or the family attorney.

Ken Bitticks

Acknowledgments

We wish to express our heartfelt gratitude to the following people who helped make this book possible.

To Debby's family, from Debby: Special gratitude to my husband Ken who was constantly supportive with endless enthusiasm to see this project through, and to our children, Shari, Michelle, Lynn, Sandi, Bryan, Tracey and Kevin, and their partners, CJ, Rick, Steven, J.T., Tamara, John and Citlali, who were all devoted and supportive in their care giving and the development of *The Senior Organizer.* Thank you also to all of our precious grandchildren for the love, respect and kindness you have given to your grandparents and great-grandparents.

To Lynn's family, from Lynn: To my husband Steven for the tremendous love, faith and support you gave in seeing this book through, and to my daughters, Alana and Jenna, for your patience and inspiration so I could create systems to keep our families prepared and organized.

To Dorothy's family, from Dorothy: To my dad, I'm sorry we didn't have this book available in your lifetime. It would have brought stability to our lives in the face of your own declining health. To my mom who devotes her life to "good health" for herself and others—you amaze me. Thank you Edward, Christiana and Patricia for your constant support of me and my drive to make a difference in the world.

To our staff: We all thank you for your powerful leadership each day in the areas for which you are responsible. Thank you for leading all of us so masterfully! Angie, we are grateful for your devotion to our bottom line; Chris, for always going the extra mile for our clients; Gillian, for your facilitation of every aspect of our company; Jean, for always knowing what to do; Jeanette, for stepping in as our "director of first impressions"; Jerry, for being our Mac genius; Johnny, for your creative and versatile leadership; and Pat, for acting as our "on-call" research department. David, our companies could not function without your consistency, diplomacy and integrity.

To our publisher, Peter Vegso, thank you for believing in us a second time. Whenever we think or say your name, we feel joy and gratitude. To those of you who are accountable to edit, market, coordinate, connect, collect, make, ship, represent or sell our books: Pat Holdsworth, Kim Weiss, Elisabeth Rinaldi, Julie De La Cruz and Lori Golden and all the people whose names we do not know but who tirelessly work

Acknowledgments

toward our success, we rest more easily each night knowing who you are for us.

To our teachers and mentors: Oh dear, the things we didn't know. Thank you for exercising extreme patience and teaching us each and every time we met with you: Linnae Andersen, Patty Aubery, David Boyd, Tom Epley, Marty and Judy Feldman, Jim Freedman, Steve Green, Russ Kamalski, Candace Shivers Morgen and Larry Thomas.

To our sources of inspiration: Your passion and motivation inspire us and everyone with whom we come in contact. Each day we connect with one of you through prayer, your books, on the phone or using the tools you have taught us. Thank you Raymond Bitticks, Jack Canfield, Mark Victor Hansen, Dr. Phil McGraw, Tom Peters, Michael Reagan, Tony Robbins, Rabbi Meier Schimmel and Selma Schimmel.

To our experts: You are our guides. We deeply appreciate and heavily rely upon your intelligence and credibility, and thank you for allowing us to reach the public through your participation in our quest to make the world a safer place. Thank you, Dr. Abdelmonem Afifi, Sharma Bennett, Dennis Bogard, LAPD Chief Willam Bratton, Rick Cataldo, Brad Dotts, Dr. Jonathan Fielding, Sandra Goroff, Donna Griggs, Nils Grevilius, Chuck Hurewitz, Halina Irving M.S., M.F.T., Pam Kelly, Chris Kingry, Deborah Lebovits, Phil Lobel, Barbara Massey, Rochelle Maurer, Dr. Sanjaya Saxena, Jeff Scott, Dr. Marion Sommers, Sari Steele and Steve Weiner.

To our business affiliations: The organizations to which we belong support our ever-growing businesses. The opportunities you present to us allow us to learn more about our business. Thank you, National Association of Professional Organizers (NAPO), National Study Group on Chronic Disorganization (NSGCD), National Association of Women Business Owners (NAWBO), National Association of Female Executives (NAFE), Small Business Association (SBA), Los Angeles Chamber of Commerce, the National Council on the Aging (NCOA).

How to Use
The Senior Organizer

The Senior Organizer helps you assemble your own or your loved one's important personal, medical, religious, legal and financial information in a simple format. When using this book, you'll be able to answer important questions and handle crucial tasks with confidence and efficiency at times when every minute may count dearly.

The Senior Organizer is divided into two parts. Part One covers personal and medical data, and Part Two deals with legal and financial information. A number of pages in Part Two are marked "Confidential" because they may contain sensitive information once you have completed them. To keep such information private and protected from identity theft, we suggest that you remove these pages from the book. Alternatively, you could make a copy of the page, complete and file it in a confidential location, and write on the page in the book who has this important information, or where it is located.

Due to changing life circumstances (for example, changing medications), we suggest you complete this book in pencil to enable you to update it easily.

You may find it useful to purchase a binder and make two copies of the pages that you plan to use from *The Senior Organizer*; keep one of them as a master and fill out the second one. The second copy can then be kept in the binder.

Alternatively, go to our Web site, *www.biobinders.com/forms*, click on the icon "Senior Organizer Forms," and type in the requested information along with the access code. (You will find the access code at the bottom of each form in this book.) A confirmation message containing the link to download free forms for your own personal use will be emailed to you immediately. Placing these forms in a binder will enable you to keep additional important documents and pertinent paperwork in the same place.

Whether you complete the book, make copies, or download forms and place them in a binder, all your information is now portable. For example, when going to a doctor's appointment, this book provides extremely important information that can make a tremendous difference in your health care. In the event of a medical emergency, once again, having this critical information immediately accessible can literally save your life.

Whether used daily or only in times of emergency, *The Senior Organizer* is an all-in-one source of personal, medical, religious, legal and financial information that can save you time and money—and maybe even a life.

Part I

Personal & Medical

Emergency & Doctor Visit Information

The more information a patient can give doctors and nurses the better they are able to help. Organizing this Emergency & Doctor Visit Information section will better inform medical personnel, whether in an emergency or routine exam, and help with speedy diagnosis and subsequent treatment.

In times of emergency, you'll need to have crucial information at your fingertips. Fill out this "Emergency Information" form completely and keep it up to date.

IN CASE OF EMERGENCY, DIAL 9-1-1

Senior Information

This *Senior Organizer* belongs to:

Name: _____

Address: _____

Phone Number: _____

Date of Birth: _____

Social Security #: _____

Other Information: _____

_____

Emergency Information

Emergency Contacts:

Name:

_____

Relationship to Senior:

_____

Phone Number(s):

_____(work)

_____ (home)

_____ (mobile)

Name:

_____

Relationship to Senior:

_____

Phone Number(s):

_____(work)

_____ (home)

_____ (mobile)

Name:

_____

Relationship to Senior:

_____

Phone Number(s):

_____(work)

_____ (home)

_____ (mobile)

Name:

_____

Relationship to Senior:

_____

Phone Number(s):

_____(work)

_____ (home)

_____ (mobile)

Location of nearest hospital:

Name of hospital: _____

Address: _____

Phone #: _____

Directions to hospital from home: _____

_____

_____

Emergency Information

Primary Health Insurance Carrier:

Name of company: _____

Patient's ID #: _____

Phone # of insurance co.: _____

> Attach copy of
>
> Health Insurance card

Secondary Health Insurance Carrier (if any):

Name of company: _____

Patient's ID #: _____

Phone # of insurance co.: _____

> Attach copy of
>
> Health Insurance card

Emergency Information

Primary Care Physician:

Name of company: _____

Name: _____

Address: _____

_____

_____

Phone Number: _____

Fax Number: _____

E-mail: _____

Blood Type: _____

Allergies to medications/known drug interactions:

_____

_____

_____

_____

_____

_____

Allergies to foods or other substances:

_____

_____

_____

_____

_____

_____

Medications / Pharmacy Information

Some people take as many as 25–30 medications a day! Any of these medicines may interact with food, drink or other medications, and *all* have the potential to cause side effects, some of which can be life-threatening. Therefore, it's absolutely essential to keep accurate records of all the medications the senior is currently taking—even aspirin!

Use the "Medications/Pharmacy Information" forms that follow to list all prescription and over-the-counter medications currently being taken, plus those that were discontinued within the past six months. Include:

- dosage
- number of times taken per day
- date medication was started
- date medication was discontinued (if any)
- side effects or reactions

Purchasing a medication dispenser box may prove to be very beneficial, as keeping track of numerous medications can be challenging. Should you choose to use a weekly medication box it is recommended that you go through all the medicines on a weekly basis, ahead of time, and place the prescribed dosages in the appropriate boxes. It is, of course, critical that this is done correctly, as an error could result in a tragic situation.

Either way it may be advantageous to write up a master sheet, especially for a caregiver, explaining which medications go in which boxes each day, writing the name of the drug, what it is for and perhaps the color of the pill to help differentiate from the others. If using this method, it is crucial to make sure that your master sheet is *always* updated as prescriptions or dosages change; for this reason it is suggested that you write your master sheet with a pencil.

Note: A prescription number could change if the medication is not reordered within the expected refill time.

Medications / Pharmacy Information

Name of medication:

_____

Doctor who prescribed medication:

_____

Reason medication prescribed:

_____

Date medication started:

_____

Dosage:

_____

Times taken per day:

_____

Side effects experienced:

_____

Date medication discontinued (if any):

_____

Reason for discontinuing
medication, if no longer taking it:

_____

Where medication is located:

_____

Pharmacy Information:

Name: _____

Prescription #: _____

Contact Person: _____

Address: _____

Phone Number: _____

Fax Number: _____

E-mail: _____

Web site: _____

Medications / Pharmacy Information

Name of medication:

_____

Reason medication prescribed:

_____

Dosage:

_____

Side effects experienced:

_____

Reason for discontinuing
medication, if no longer taking it:

_____

Doctor who prescribed medication:

_____

Date medication started:

_____

Times taken per day:

_____

Date medication discontinued (if any):

_____

Where medication is located:

_____

Pharmacy Information:

Name: _____

Prescription #: _____

Contact Person: _____

Address: _____

Phone Number: _____

Fax Number: _____

E-mail: _____

Web site: _____

Medications / Pharmacy Information

Name of medication:

_____

Doctor who prescribed medication:

_____

Reason medication prescribed:

_____

Date medication started:

_____

Dosage:

_____

Times taken per day:

_____

Side effects experienced:

_____

Date medication discontinued (if any):

_____

Reason for discontinuing
medication, if no longer taking it:

_____

Where medication is located:

_____

Pharmacy Information:

Name: _____

Prescription #: _____

Contact Person: _____

Address: _____

Phone Number: _____

Fax Number: _____

E-mail: _____

Web site: _____

Medications / Pharmacy Information

Name of medication:

_____

Reason medication prescribed:

_____

Dosage:

_____

Side effects experienced:

_____

Reason for discontinuing
medication, if no longer taking it:

_____

Doctor who prescribed medication:

_____

Date medication started:

_____

Times taken per day:

_____

Date medication discontinued (if any):

_____

Where medication is located:

_____

Pharmacy Information:

Name: _____

Prescription #: _____

Contact Person: _____

Address: _____

Phone Number: _____

Fax Number: _____

E-mail: _____

Web site: _____

Medications / Pharmacy Information

Name of medication:

_____

Reason medication prescribed:

_____

Dosage:

_____

Side effects experienced:

_____

Reason for discontinuing
medication, if no longer taking it:

_____

Doctor who prescribed medication:

_____

Date medication started:

_____

Times taken per day:

_____

Date medication discontinued (if any):

_____

Where medication is located:

_____

Pharmacy Information:

Name: _____

Prescription #: _____

Contact Person: _____

Address: _____

Phone Number: _____

Fax Number: _____

E-mail: _____

Web site: _____

Medications / Pharmacy Information

Name of medication:

_____

Doctor who prescribed medication:

_____

Reason medication prescribed:

_____

Date medication started:

_____

Dosage:

_____

Times taken per day:

_____

Side effects experienced:

_____

Date medication discontinued (if any):

_____

Reason for discontinuing
medication, if no longer taking it:

_____

Where medication is located:

_____

Pharmacy Information:

Name: _____

Prescription #: _____

Contact Person: _____

Address: _____

Phone Number: _____

Fax Number: _____

E-mail: _____

Web site: _____

Herbs, Vitamins & Other Supplements

Even though they're considered "natural," herbs, vitamins and other supplements may interact with medications or each other to produce side effects—some of which can be quite dangerous. For example, vitamin E can increase the risk of uncontrolled bleeding, licorice root can work against the effects of high blood pressure medications, and St. John's Wort combined with antidepressant drugs can be deadly. For this reason always inform members of the medical profession when taking any kind of "natural" supplement.

Use the "Herbs, Vitamins & Other Supplements" forms that follow to keep careful track of all the herbs, vitamins and other supplements. List all herbs, vitamins or other supplements currently taken, plus those that were discontinued within the past six months.

Be sure to keep this list up to date.

Herbs, Vitamins & Other Supplements

Name of Herb, Vitamin or Supplement

Name: _____

Brand name: Potency:

_____   _____

Date started: Date discontinued (if no longer taking it):

_____   _____

Times taken per day: _____

Reason for taking it: _____

_____

_____

_____

Side effects experienced: _____

_____

_____

_____

Reason for discontinuing (if no longer taking it): _____

_____

_____

_____

Herbs, Vitamins & Other Supplements

Name of Herb, Vitamin or Supplement

Name: _____

Brand name: Potency:

_____   _____

Date started: Date discontinued (if no longer taking it):

_____   _____

Times taken per day: _____

Reason for taking it: _____

_____

_____

_____

Side effects experienced: _____

_____

_____

_____

Reason for discontinuing (if no longer taking it): _____

_____

_____

_____

Current Health Issues & Medical History

A thorough medical history can play a crucial role in the accurate diagnosis and treatment of an illness or dealing with an emergency. Health care professionals have long known that common diseases and even some rare ones can be hereditary.

In 2004 Thanksgiving Day was declared to be the first annual National Family History Day by the U.S. Surgeon General Richard H. Carmona M.D., M.P.H., who encourages everyone to discuss and keep records of any health problems within their family. Learning about a family's health history can be a powerful tool for predicting illness and ensuring a longer future together, and it is extremely important that a medical history be recorded as accurately and completely as possible.

On the "Current Health Issues" form, write down problems that are currently an issue, including the length of time the problems have existed. Go through all medical files, and request medical records from health care providers; fill out the "Medical History" form that follows as completely and accurately as possible. Be sure to include any allergies.

If eyeglasses are currently being worn, it is a good idea to keep a copy of the prescription together with a record of the optometrist who performed the examination, just in case you break, lose or decide to replace your glasses. An eyeglass prescription can only be filled within one year of the date it was written, so it is advisable to have your doctor rewrite the old one each year even if you do not get your eyes tested or your prescription does not change.

In this subsection you will find:

- Current Health Issues
- Medical History
- Family's Medical History
- Eyeglass Information

Current Health Issues

Do you smoke cigarettes or have you ever smoked cigarettes? _____

If so, how long? _____

How many packs a day do/did you smoke?_____

Do you drink alcohol? _____

If so, how much per day?_____

Please list ALL allergies you have, especially to medications, e.g., Penicillin.

_____

_____

_____

Please check only if you have any of the following symptoms:

_____ Loss of Hair

_____ Hearing Difficulty

_____ Shortness of Breath

_____ Arthritis

_____ Headache

_____ Swelling in Neck

_____ Double Vision

_____ Blind Spots

_____ Cataracts

_____ Pain in Eyes

_____ Dizziness

_____ Lightheadedness

_____ Fainting Spells

_____ Dry Eyes

_____ Weakness/Numbness
in Any One Area
of the Body

_____ Leg Cramps when
Walking

_____ Nervous Depression

_____ Weight Loss

_____ Abdominal Pain

_____ Black/Tarry Bowel
Movements

_____ Irregular Menses

_____ Impotence

_____ Blood in Urine

_____ Frequent Urination

_____ Change in Thickness
of Stools

_____ Burning with Urination

_____ Constipation

_____ Sinus Problems

_____ Gum Infections

_____ Heat Intolerance

_____ Cold Intolerance

_____ Weight Gain

_____ Palpitations

_____ Stroke

_____ Cough

_____ Dry Mouth

_____ Difficulty Swallowing

_____ Asthma

_____ Nose Bleeds

_____ Frequent Thirst

_____ Sore Tongue

_____ Chest Pain

_____ Pain in Ears

_____ Roaring in Ears

Current Health Issues

Name of illness or medical problem: _____

_____

How long has problem existed? _____

_____

_____

_____

Current treatments: _____

_____

_____

_____

Outcome: _____

_____

_____

Name of illness or medical problem: _____

_____

How long has problem existed? _____

_____

_____

_____

Current treatments: _____

_____

_____

_____

Outcome: _____

_____

Current Health Issues

Name of illness or medical problem: _____

_____

How long has problem existed? _____

_____

_____

_____

Current treatments: _____

_____

_____

_____

Outcome: _____

_____

_____

Name of illness or medical problem: _____

_____

How long has problem existed? _____

_____

_____

_____

Current treatments: _____

_____

_____

_____

Outcome: _____

_____

Current Health Issues

Name of illness or medical problem: _____

_____

How long has problem existed? _____

_____

_____

_____

Current treatments: _____

_____

_____

_____

Outcome: _____

_____

_____

Name of illness or medical problem: _____

_____

How long has problem existed? _____

_____

_____

_____

Current treatments: _____

_____

_____

_____

Outcome: _____

_____

Medical History

Health Questions

Describe medical attention received (where and when), and also date of onset. ___

_____

_____

_____

_____

_____

Please list any serious accidents or injuries that you've experienced.

_____

_____

_____

_____

_____

Please list any serious illnesses that you experienced.

_____

_____

_____

_____

_____

_____

Copy this form or download it from *www.biobinders.com/forms*, access code: soforms

Medical History

Were you ever hospitalized? _____ If so, please list the reason, date and length of stay for each hospitalization.

_____

_____

_____

_____

_____

_____

_____

Have you ever had surgery? _____ If so, please list the reasons.

_____

_____

_____

_____

_____

_____

Do you have any genetic diseases? _____ If so, please list each one, its symptoms, and tell how you discovered that you had this disease. _____

_____

_____

_____

_____

_____

Medical History

Have you ever undergone any genetic testing? _____ If yes, what were the results?

_____

_____

_____

Do you have any history of high/low blood pressure? _____ If so, which one, and what was the highest or lowest number that it reached?

_____

_____

Do you have any history of high cholesterol? _____ If so, do you know any of your lab values (i.e., total cholesterol, LDH, HDL)? List them if possible. _____

_____

_____

_____

Do you have any history of heart disease? _____ If so, please explain.

_____

_____

_____

Do you have any history of strokes? _____ If so, please explain.

_____

_____

_____

Do you have any history of cancer? _____ If so, please explain.

_____

_____

_____

Medical History

Do you have any history of diabetes? _____ If so, was it juvenile-onset or adult-onset?

_____

_____

Do you have any history of skin conditions? _____ If so, please explain.

_____

_____

_____

Have you experienced depression or any other mental health challenge(s) during your lifetime? If so, please explain. _____

_____

_____

_____

Do you have any other significant medical conditions? _____

_____

_____

_____

Please list last dates of immunizations/shots. _____

_____

_____

_____

_____

Miscellaneous: Please list anything else you think might be of value._____

_____

_____

_____

_____

Medical History

Family Health History

When gathering your family's health history you may also want to visit the U.S. Surgeon General's Web site at www.hhs.gov/familyhistory/ to help you identify common diseases that may run in your family. The list that follows may also help you.

Do you know of any BLOOD RELATIVE who has or had any of the following?
(Please give your relationship to the person):

	Relationship	Age of Onset
___ High Blood Pressure:	_____	_____
___ Low Blood Pressure:	_____	_____
___ High Cholesterol:	_____	_____
___ Stroke:	_____	_____
___ Diabetes:	_____	_____
___ Heart Disease:	_____	_____
___ Macular Degeneration:	_____	_____
___ Colon Cancer:	_____	_____
___ Breast Cancer:	_____	_____
___ Ovarian Cancer:	_____	_____
___ Cancer (other):	_____	_____
___ Other:	_____	_____
___ Other:	_____	_____
___ Other:	_____	_____
___ Other:	_____	_____

Eyeglass Information

Name of Optometrist:_____

Address: _____

_____

Phone: _____ Fax: _____

E-mail: _____

Other: _____

_____

Name of Optometrist:_____

Address: _____

_____

Phone: _____ Fax: _____

E-mail: _____

Other: _____

_____

(Attach a copy of Eyeglass Prescription)

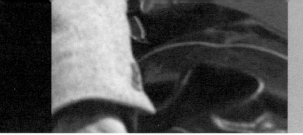

Items for Emergency Overnight Bag

Having a bag already packed can be extremely helpful in case of an emergency hospitalization. This bag should contain at least a couple of pairs of pajamas, some underwear, some comfortable street clothes to wear home, plus any personal care items that may be needed. Some of these items can be packed in advance, while others will have to be added at the last minute.

Use the following sample list to help you create your own packing list.

Packed Bag
- 2 pair pajamas
- 1 robe/slippers
- 2 shirts
- 2 pair trousers
- 1 sweater
- 7 pair underwear
- toothbrush & toothpaste
- deodorant
- body/face lotion
- comb/brush
- eyeglasses
- religious items, including any dietary restrictions
- Durable Power of Attorney for Health/Advance Directives (signed)

Add to bag when leaving
- ALL medications
- Your *Senior Organizer*
- Wallet/purse
- Address book
- Original insurance card
- Hearing aid
- Dentures

List everything the senior will need to have in his or her overnight bag on the "Items for the Overnight Bag" form that follows. Remember to check bag regularly for any outdated items, and make changes accordingly.

Items for Emergency Overnight Bag

Already packed:

_____
_____
_____
_____
_____
_____
_____
_____
_____
_____
_____
_____

Items to add:

_____
_____
_____
_____
_____
_____
_____
_____
_____
_____
_____
_____
_____

Personal Information

It's important to have easy access to basic personal information, including birth date, Social Security, driver's license and/or identification numbers, names of family members, and so on.

Some of this information is repeated from the "Emergency Information" page, but here you'll have the space to write out full addresses, phone numbers, fax numbers and other information. Important medical information can also be listed briefly here.

Fill out the "Basic Personal Information" form that follows, and update it as needed.

If you prefer not to jot down the Social Security number or other personal information, be sure to write the name of the person who has that information or where it can be located.

Basic Personal Information

Name: _____

Home Address (where currently residing): _____

_____

_____

Home Phone: _____   Mobile Phone: _____

Fax Number: _____   E-mail: _____

Social Security #: _____   Date of Birth: _____

Driver's Lic. #: _____   ID Card #: _____

State: _____   Expiration Date: _____

Where to find the driver's license or ID card: _____

_____

_____

Attach copy of

Driver's License or ID Card

Health Insurance Carrier(s)

Primary Health Insurance Carrier:

Name of company: _____

_____

_____

Address: _____

_____

_____

Phone #: _____

Your ID #: _____

_____

Where to find this card: _____

_____

_____

Attach copy of

Health Insurance card

Copy this form or download it from *www.biobinders.com/forms*, access code: soforms

Health Insurance Carrier(s)

Secondary Health Insurance Carrier (if any):

Name of company: _____

_____

_____

Address: _____

_____

_____

Phone #: _____

Your ID #: _____

_____

Where to find this card: _____

_____

_____

Attach copy of

Health Insurance card

Health Insurance Carrier(s)

Additional Health Insurance Carrier (if any):

Name of company: _____

_____

_____

Address: _____

_____

_____

Phone #: _____

Your ID #: _____

_____

Where to find this card: _____

_____

_____

Attach copy of

Health Insurance card

Contact Information for Spouse/Significant Other

(if any)

Name: _____

Address: _____

_____

_____

Relationship to Person: _____

_____

Phone Number(s): _____

_____

E-mail: _____

Other Information: _____

_____

_____

_____

_____

_____

_____

_____

_____

_____

_____

Family Members/Friends
to be contacted in case of emergency

Name: _____

Address: _____

_____

_____

Relationship to Person: _____

_____

Phone Number(s): _____

_____

E-mail: _____

Other Information: _____

_____

Name: _____

Address: _____

_____

_____

Relationship to Person: _____

_____

Phone Number(s): _____

_____

E-mail: _____

Other Information: _____

_____

Family Members/Friends
to be contacted in case
of emergency

Name: _____

Address: _____

_____

_____

Relationship to Person: _____

_____

Phone Number(s): _____

_____

E-mail: _____

Other Information: _____

_____

Name: _____

Address: _____

_____

_____

Relationship to Person: _____

_____

Phone Number(s): _____

_____

E-mail: _____

Other Information: _____

_____

Organization Memberships

Name of organization: _____

_____

_____

Address: _____

_____

_____

Phone #: _____

Your ID #: _____

Member Since: _____

Membership Renewal Date: _____

Other: _____

_____

Attach copy of

Membership card

Organization Memberships

Name of organization: _____

_____

_____

Address: _____

_____

_____

Phone #: _____

Your ID #: _____

Member Since: _____

Membership Renewal Date: _____

Other: _____

_____

Attach copy of

Membership card

Organization Memberships

Name of organization: _____

_____

_____

Address: _____

_____

_____

Phone #: _____

Your ID #: _____

Member Since: _____

Membership Renewal Date: _____

Other: _____

_____

Attach copy of

Membership card

Medical Information

It can be hard to keep track of the many different medical practitioners and/or other health care providers who might be part of a senior's health care team, especially with the increasing use of "alternative" health care professionals.

This Medical Information Section contains the following subsections, each of which is designed to help you document the various aspects of a senior's health care.

- Physicians' Information
- Other Health Care Providers
- Medical Facility Stays
- Getting the Most Out of Medical Appointments
- Health Tracking Sheets

Please note: Medications, pharmacy contact information, current health issues and health history information are all in the "Emergency and Doctor Visit Information' section.

Physicians' Information

Write the name and contact information for each physician on the "Physicians' Information" form, noting his or her specialty and the reason for consultation.

Name of Doctor: _____

_____

Specialty/Reasons for Consult: _____

_____

Address: _____

_____

_____

Phone: _____ Fax: _____

E-mail:_____ Other: _____

Name of Doctor: _____

_____

Specialty/Reasons for Consult: _____

_____

Address: _____

_____

_____

Phone: _____ Fax: _____

E-mail:_____ Other: _____

Copy this form or download it from *www.biobinders.com/forms*, access code: soforms

Physicians' Information

Name of Doctor: _____

_____

Specialty/Reasons for Consult: _____

_____

Address: _____

_____

_____

Phone: _____ Fax: _____

E-mail: _____ Other: _____

Name of Doctor: _____

_____

Specialty/Reasons for Consult: _____

_____

Address: _____

_____

_____

Phone: _____ Fax: _____

E-mail: _____ Other: _____

Physicians' Information

Name of Doctor: _____

_____

Specialty/Reasons for Consult: _____

_____

Address: _____

_____

_____

Phone: _____ Fax: _____

E-mail:_____ Other: _____

Name of Doctor: _____

_____

Specialty/Reasons for Consult: _____

_____

Address: _____

_____

_____

Phone: _____ Fax: _____

E-mail:_____ Other: _____

Copy this form or download it from *www.biobinders.com/forms*, access code: soforms

Other Health Care Providers

More and more frequently "alternative" health care is combined with traditional, and it is advisable to keep records of all those providers as well.

Name of Doctor: _____

_____

Specialty/Reasons for Consult: _____

_____

Address: _____

_____

_____

Phone: _____ Fax: _____

E-mail:_____ Other: _____

Name of Doctor: _____

_____

Specialty/Reasons for Consult: _____

_____

Address: _____

_____

_____

Phone: _____ Fax: _____

E-mail:_____ Other: _____

Other Health Care Providers

Name of Doctor: _____

_____

Specialty/Reasons for Consult: _____

_____

Address: _____

_____

_____

Phone: _____ Fax: _____

E-mail:_____ Other: _____

Name of Doctor: _____

_____

Specialty/Reasons for Consult: _____

_____

Address: _____

_____

_____

Phone: _____ Fax: _____

E-mail:_____ Other: _____

Copy this form or download it from *www.biobinders.com/forms*, access code: soforms

Other Health Care Providers

Name of Doctor: _____

_____

Specialty/Reasons for Consult: _____

_____

Address: _____

_____

_____

Phone: _____   Fax: _____

E-mail:_____   Other: _____

Name of Doctor: _____

_____

Specialty/Reasons for Consult: _____

_____

Address: _____

_____

_____

Phone: _____   Fax: _____

E-mail:_____   Other: _____

Medical Facility Stays

A senior may go to various hospitals, rehabilitation facilities and/or nursing homes. It can be difficult to remember when and why these stays occurred, and what happened each time.

Use the forms in this section to record the history of each hospital, nursing home or rehabilitation facility stay together with the document holders to keep the originals or copies of any admittance and/or discharge paperwork. Each tracking sheet should include the reason for admittance; arrival and departure dates; outcome; names and positions of key caregivers; any procedures that have been recommended as well as driving directions to the facility.

In this section you will find the following subsections:

- "Hospital Stay" form
- "Nursing Home Stay" form
- "Rehabilitation Facility Stay" form

Medical Facility Stays

Hospital Stay

(Make sure to save a copy of your nursing home paperwork.)

Name of Hospital: _____

Hospital address: _____

_____

_____

_____

Reason for admittance: _____   Dates of stay: _____

Phone number: _____   Fax number: _____

Names & positions of key caregivers/contacts at hospital: _____

_____

_____

_____

_____

Driving directions from home: _____

_____

_____

Comments/follow-up care instructions: _____

_____

_____

_____

_____

_____

Medical Facility Stays

Nursing Home Stay

(Make sure to save a copy of your hospital paperwork.)

Name of Nursing Home: _____

Nursing Home address: _____

_____

_____

_____

Reason for admittance: _____   Dates of stay: _____

Phone number: _____   Fax number: _____

Names & positions of key caregivers/contacts at nursing home: _____

_____

_____

_____

_____

Driving directions from home: _____

_____

_____

Comments/follow-up care instructions: _____

_____

_____

_____

_____

_____

Medical Facility Stays

Rehabilitation Facility Stay

(Make sure to save a copy of your rehab facility paperwork.)

Name of Rehabilitation Facility: _____

Rehabilitation Facility address: _____

_____

_____

_____

Reason for admittance: _____ Dates of stay: _____

_____ _____

Phone number: _____ Fax number: _____

_____ _____

Names & positions of key caregivers/contacts at rehabilitation facility: _____

_____

_____

_____

_____

Driving directions from home: _____

_____

_____

_____

Comments/follow-up care instructions: _____

_____

_____

_____

_____

_____

Getting the Most Out of Medical Appointments

Doctors typically spend precious little time with their patients; therefore, it's important that this time be well-spent. This means doing a little preparation beforehand, so that you can arrive with all pertinent information in hand.

Filling out the health and medical information in this book completely and bringing it along to all doctor appointments is a great start.

You can also request copies of the pertinent medical records, including the results of laboratory studies and other tests, procedures and/or surgeries. Doing so will help you to become thoroughly familiar with the medical history, and aid you in filling out *The Senior Organizer* more accurately. It will also save time when going to new doctors who don't have copies of all the relevant records.

Many people have questions they want to ask the doctor, but forget to ask them—or some of them—during the appointment. Thus, the time with the doctor can be made even more productive if you write out your questions on the "Getting the Most Out of Medical Appointments" form in advance. The doctor's answers, plus the patient's blood pressure, weight, pulse and the results of other tests performed in the office, can also be recorded on this form. *(Be sure to take a fresh form to each new doctor's appointment for your record keeping.)*

The "Health Tracking Sheets" at the end of the Medical Information section will help you provide answers to questions that your doctor may have about symptoms or reactions. (Photocopy the "Getting the Most Out of Medical Appointments" forms as needed, or go to *www.biobinders.com* to download more forms.)

Getting the Most Out of Medical Appointments

Date: _____

Health Care Provider's Name: _____

_____

Phone: _____

Reason for Appointment: _____

_____

_____

Question for Health Care Provider:

1. _____

_____

_____

_____

Health Care Provider's Answer:

_____

_____

_____

_____

Question for Health Care Provider:

2. _____

_____

_____

_____

Health Care Provider's Answer:

_____

_____

_____

_____

Getting the Most Out of Medical Appointments

Question for Health Care Provider:

3. _____

_____

_____

_____

Health Care Provider's Answer:

_____

_____

_____

_____

Question for Health Care Provider:

4. _____

_____

_____

_____

Health Care Provider's Answer:

_____

_____

_____

_____

Ask for the following information during your visit:

Basic Vital Signs

Temperature: _____

Blood Pressure: _____

Pulse: _____

Copy this form or download it from *www.biobinders.com/forms*, access code: soforms

Getting the Most Out of Medical Appointments

Other information:

Results of prior tests:

_____

_____

_____

_____

_____

When will results of today's tests be available?

_____

_____

_____

_____

What treatment are you recommending?

_____

_____

_____

_____

What are the pros & cons of this treatment?

_____

_____

_____

_____

Getting the Most Out of Medical Appointments

How long will this treatment continue?

_____
_____
_____

What can I do to help make the treatment most effective?

_____
_____
_____
_____
_____

What are the alternatives to this treatment?

_____
_____
_____
_____
_____
_____
_____
_____
_____
_____
_____
_____
_____

Health Tracking Sheets

A health care provider is likely to ask "When did this symptom first show up?" or "Were there any reactions to this medication?" or "How much liquid is being consumed?" It can be hard to give accurate answers unless good records have been kept.

The "Health Tracking Sheets" that follow make it easy to record symptoms, reactions to medication, food/liquid consumption, weight, mood and other items on a daily, weekly or monthly basis. The "Health Tracking Sheets" are particularly helpful for recording:

- severity of symptoms from day to day
- reactions to medications or other treatments
- test results
- emotional reactions (anxiety, depression, irritability, etc.)
- food and liquid consumption

Make photocopies of the "Health Tracking Sheets" or go to *www.biobinders.com* to download them as needed, and fill them out regularly. Be sure to bring the sheets to all medical appointments.

In this section you will find the following subsections:

- "Daily Health Tracking Sheet"
- "Weekly Health Tracking Sheet"
- "Monthly Health Tracking Sheet"

Health Tracking Sheets

Daily Health Tracking Sheet

Name: _____ Date: _____

Completed by: _____

What are you tracking (for example: symptoms, reactions to medication, food/liquid consumption, weight, mood, etc.)?

_____

_____

6:00am	_____
7:00am	_____
8:00am	_____
9:00am	_____
10:00am	_____
11:00am	_____
12:00pm	_____
1:00pm	_____
2:00pm	_____
3:00pm	_____
4:00pm	_____
5:00pm	_____
6:00pm	_____
7:00pm	_____
8:00pm	_____
9:00pm	_____
10:00pm	_____
11:00pm	_____
12:00am	_____
1:00am	_____
2:00am	_____
3:00am	_____
4:00am	_____
5:00am	_____

Health Tracking Sheets

Weekly Health Tracking Sheet

Name: _____   Week of: _____

Completed by: _____

_____

What are you tracking (for example: symptoms, food/liquid consumption, reactions to medication, weight, mood, etc.)?

_____

_____

_____

_____

Sunday _____

_____

Monday _____

_____

Tuesday _____

_____

Wednesday _____

_____

Thursday _____

_____

Friday _____

_____

Saturday _____

_____

Health Tracking Sheets

Monthly Health Tracking Sheet

Name: _____   Completed by: _____

What are you tracking (for example: symptoms, reactions to medication, weight, mood, etc.)?

_____

_____

_____

January _____

_____

_____

_____

February _____

_____

_____

_____

March _____

_____

_____

_____

April _____

_____

_____

_____

May _____

_____

_____

_____

Health Tracking Sheets

Monthly Tracking Sheet

June _____
_____
_____
_____

July _____
_____
_____
_____

August _____
_____
_____
_____

September _____
_____
_____
_____

October _____
_____
_____
_____

November _____
_____
_____
_____

December _____
_____
_____
_____

Personal Care

This Personal Care Section contains the following subsections, each of which is designed to help keep and maintain records for the senior regarding day-to-day life, activities, personal requirements and data.

- Daily Routine or Schedule
- Personal Grooming & Size Information
- Diet & Nutrition Information

Daily Routine/ Schedule

People tend to feel most comfortable when their lives have a certain amount of routine and structure. This can be especially true for seniors, who may feel they are "losing control" of their physical or cognitive abilities—or of their independence and autonomy.

Using the "Daily Routine/Schedule" form that follows can help keep track of day-to-day activities as well as provide a resource for a caregiver should the circumstance arise. It will give a clear idea of wants and needs, helping to maintain a schedule. Be sure to assign a time of day to each activity. Although the time may vary from day to day, for scheduling purposes pick the most likely time. Also, try to be as specific as possible in the description. For example, instead of writing "takes a nap," it is more helpful to note that "Joe likes to take a nap on the reclining chair with classical music on."

Be sure and list any rituals that may help to support and maintain a stress-free environment. For example, when getting ready for bed at night, there may be five things to do in a certain order: Put on nightclothes, wash face, brush teeth, cream on hands and read in bed for a little while. These little details can make a world of difference—and a caregiver might otherwise never know about them. Any additional details can be recorded in the "Special Notes" section of the "Daily Routine" form.

Daily Routine/ Schedule

Daily Routine

The following is a SAMPLE of a "Daily Routine" form:

Time	Activity
7:00am	Wakes up. On Monday, Wednesday and Friday, she takes a shower. On other days she just washes her face.
8:00am	Breakfast, Monday, Wednesday and Friday cereal and fruit, takes AM medications with a glass of water.
8:30am	On Tuesdays and Thursdays, she goes to Aqua Fit at YWCA. Class starts at 9:00am, ends at 10:00am. Needs help getting into and out of bathing suit. On other days of week, watches the "Morning News," then "Regis" at 9am, and "The Price Is Right" at 10am.
11:30am	Eats lunch. She likes a tuna sandwich on wheat, an orange divided into sections, and a small green salad. She eats chocolate pudding for dessert.
12 noon	Takes midday medications with a glass of water.
1:00pm	She takes a nap in her bedroom with the white noise machine on.
4:00pm	On Friday of every week goes to ballroom dancing class at community center.
6:00pm	Eats dinner. Usually has grilled chicken or beef, rice, a cooked vegetable, some canned fruit and ice cream for dessert. Takes medications (see "Medications" section under Emergency/Doctor Visit Information.)
7:00pm	Watches TV—she likes "Entertainment Tonight," "Everybody Loves Raymond" and "7th Heaven." Also likes old movies if they finish up by 9:00pm.
9:30pm	Gets into bed and reads until she falls asleep. She usually is able to sleep through the night.

Special Notes: Please put a glass of water on the nightstand next to her bed at night. Also, she sleeps with 4 pillows: two under her head, one between her knees and one supporting her back.

Daily Routine/ Schedule

Daily Routine

Time of day	Activity
7:00am	_____
	_____
	_____
7:30am	_____
	_____
	_____
8:00am	_____
	_____
	_____
8:30am	_____
	_____
	_____
9:00am	_____
	_____
	_____
9:30am	_____
	_____
	_____

Daily Routine/ Schedule

Daily Routine

Time of day	Activity
10:00am	_____
	_____
	_____
10:30am	_____
	_____
	_____
11:00am	_____
	_____
	_____
11:30am	_____
	_____
	_____
12:00pm	_____
	_____
	_____
12:30pm	_____
	_____
	_____

Daily Routine/ Schedule

Daily Routine

Time of day	Activity
1:00pm	_____
	_____
	_____
1:30pm	_____
	_____
	_____
2:00pm	_____
	_____
	_____
2:30pm	_____
	_____
	_____
3:00pm	_____
	_____
	_____
3:30pm	_____
	_____
	_____

Daily Routine/ Schedule

Daily Routine

Time of day	Activity
4:00pm	
4:30pm	
5:00pm	
5:30pm	
6:00pm	
6:30pm	

Daily Routine/ Schedule

Daily Routine

Time of day   **Activity**

7:00pm _____

_____

_____

7:30pm _____

_____

_____

8:00pm _____

_____

_____

8:30pm _____

_____

_____

9:00pm _____

_____

_____

9:30pm _____

_____

_____

Personal Care

Daily Routine/ Schedule

Daily Routine

Time of day   **Activity**

10:00pm   _____

_____

_____

10:30pm   _____

_____

_____

11:00pm   _____

_____

_____

11:30pm   _____

_____

_____

12:00am   _____

_____

_____

Special Notes: _____

_____

_____

Copy this form or download it from *www.biobinders.com/forms*, access code: soforms

Personal Grooming & Size Information

Having the "right" brand of lotion or the perfect pair of tennis shoes, or getting a haircut from that special hair dresser can do much to make a senior feel comfortable and attractive. This is information that will be important for a caregiver who won't automatically know what (or who) is "right" unless you write it down. You may also want to keep a record of certain shops that carry specific preferred items.

Use the "Personal Grooming Information" form in the first part of this section to list the brand names of favorite lotions, shampoo, perfume, makeup, after shave and so on. Use the second part of this section to write down contact information for hair stylist, manicurist or any other grooming specialists.

Use the "Clothing & Shoe Sizes" form that follows to write down clothing and shoe sizes. Favorite colors and jewelry preferences can also be listed.

Personal Grooming & Size Information

Favorite Brands of Personal Care Items

For either sex

Facial soap: _____

Face lotion: _____

Body lotion: _____

Sunblock: _____

Deodorant: _____

Toothbrush: _____

Toothpaste: _____

_____

Dental floss: _____

Hair styling product: _____

_____

Hair spray: _____

Razor: _____

Shaving cream: _____

_____

Aftershave/Perfume: _____

_____

Other: _____

Other: _____

Other: _____

Other: _____

Other: _____

Other: _____

Other: _____

Other: _____

Cosmetics

Eye makeup remover: _____

_____

Eye cream: _____

_____

Face makeup (foundation): _____

_____

Blush: _____

_____

Powder: _____

_____

Eye shadow: _____

_____

Eyebrow pencil: _____

_____

Mascara: _____

_____

Lip-liner: _____

_____

Lipstick: _____

_____

Nail polish: _____

Other: _____

Other: _____

Other: _____

Other: _____

Other: _____

Personal Grooming & Size Information

For Ladies

Hair Stylist

Name of Salon:_____

Address: _____

Phone #: _____

Manicurist

Name of Salon:_____

Address: _____

Phone #: _____

Other Grooming Specialist

Name of Salon:_____

Address: _____

Phone #: _____

Clothing & Shoe Sizes

Dress: _____	Hosiery: _____
Blouse: _____	Hat: _____
T-Shirt or Sweater: _____	Other: _____
Jacket: _____	_____
Pants: _____	_____
Jeans: _____	_____
Underwear: _____	_____
Bra: _____	_____
Socks: _____	_____
Shoes: _____	_____
Belt: _____	_____

Personal Grooming & Size Information

For Men

Hair Stylist

Name of Salon:_____

Address: _____

Phone #: _____

Manicurist

Name of Salon:_____

Address: _____

Phone #: _____

Other Grooming Specialist

Name of Salon:_____

Address: _____

Phone #: _____

Clothing & Shoe Sizes

Dress Shirt: _____	Other: _____
T-Shirt: _____	_____
Jacket: _____	_____
Pants: _____	_____
Jeans: _____	_____
Underwear: _____	_____
Socks: _____	_____
Shoes: _____	_____
Belt: _____	_____
Hat: _____	_____
Other: _____	_____

Diet & Nutrition Information

Seniors are often following special diets recommended by their doctors. They may also have allergies, food sensitivities or religious dietary guidelines to follow, or problems chewing, swallowing and/or digesting certain foods. All of us have food likes and dislikes.

Use the "Diet & Nutrition Information" form that follows to record all pertinent dietary information.

Diet & Nutrition Information

Food Allergies:

(List any foods that cause a reaction, and indicate which ones may be severe. For example, some people have a life-threatening reaction to walnuts or peanuts.)

_____

_____

_____

_____

_____

Food Sensitivities:

(List any foods that cause a reaction when eaten in large quantities. For example, some people can eat small amounts of strawberries, but large amounts produce a skin rash.)

_____

_____

_____

_____

_____

Food Likes:

(List favorite foods here.)

_____

_____

_____

_____

_____

_____

_____

Diet & Nutrition Information

Food Dislikes:
(List least-favorite foods here.)

_____

_____

_____

_____

_____

_____

_____

_____

Special diet that must be followed:
(Has the doctor recommended a low-salt diet? A low-fat diet? Or some other dietary restrictions? Are there any religious dietary restrictions that must be observed? List any dietary rules and regulations here.)

_____

_____

_____

_____

_____

_____

_____

_____

_____

_____

_____

_____

_____

_____

At Home

This At Home Section contains the following subsections, each of which is designed to help keep the senior's home safe and running smoothly. Maintaining accurate records of household repairs and keeping track of items and their location within the home can be extremely helpful.

Any routine or unique information about pets can assist a caregiver and put the senior's mind at rest if they ever have to be absent from their home and need to have someone care for their pet(s).

Each subsection has its own introductory paragraph and instructions.

- Safety Precautions
- Home Safety Checklist
- Location of Items at Home
- Pet Care Information
- Repair & Maintenance Information

Safety Precautions

Safety in the home is of importance to us all, but a senior may have specific safety issues that a caregiver should be aware of—before the problem occurs and in this event a list can be very helpful.

The following list is a sample list of some items that a caregiver might need to know about:

- unsteady when going up and down stairs.

- poor night vision.

- extremely allergic to walnuts.

- likely to wander out of the house, so doors should be locked at all times.

Use the "Safety Precautions" form that follows to list any potentially dangerous situations that caregivers should know about.

Safety Precautions

Safety Precautions

1. _____
2. _____
3. _____
4. _____
5. _____
6. _____
7. _____
8. _____
9. _____
10. _____
11. _____
12. _____
13. _____
14. _____
15. _____
16. _____

Other: _____

_____

_____

_____

_____

_____

_____

_____

_____

Home Safety Checklist

Safety is important for everyone, but can be even more crucial to the senior who is unsteady on his or her feet or not as cognitively aware as he or she was in the past. Making sure floors aren't slippery, attending to loose wires and keeping all areas well-lighted are just a few of the safety precautions that everyone should take.

Take the time to consult with an expert who has experience working with seniors and get advice about any additions or changes that might improve the premises to ensure that everything is safe, such as installing hand rails next to the toilet and shower or night lights throughout the home.

Use the "Home Safety Checklist" that follows to get you started when making the home or living environment as safe as possible. For more information about a safe home environment you might want to look at the AARP Web site and read their information on "Home Safety Checklists."

Home Safety Checklist

Home Safety Checklist

(This checklist is not intended to be comprehensive. Always consult with an expert should you have any doubts or questions.)

Items to be checked	Checked/Fixed
___ Are there any frayed, cracked cords or loose wires?	_____
___ Are cords attached to the walls or baseboards with tape instead of nails or staples?	_____
___ Are there any cords stretched across walkways that could cause someone to trip?	_____
___ Are the carpets sturdy and stretched flat to the floor?	_____
___ Are all mats, rugs and runners slip-resistant?	_____
___ Are there slip-resistant mats on potentially slippery areas of the floor (especially during rainy weather)?	_____
___ Are properly functioning smoke-detectors placed near every bedroom and on every floor of the house?	_____
___ Are space heaters placed away from walkways and flammable items like drapes, furniture, rugs and bedding?	_____
___ Are all walkways, halls and heavily trafficked areas well-lit?	_____
___ Are there strong, sturdy grab bars installed next to the toilet and in the bathtub/shower area?	_____
___ Are there non-skid mats or abrasive strips installed in bathtubs and showers to ensure that they're not slippery?	_____
___ Is there a sturdy seat in the shower?	_____
___ Is the maximum water temperature less than 120 degrees?	_____
___ Are there light switches or lamps easily reached from the bed?	_____

Copy this form or download it from *www.biobinders.com/forms*, access code: soforms

Home Safety Checklist

Home Safety Checklist

Items to be checked   Checked/Fixed

___ Are all medications in their proper containers and in a safe place? _____

___ Are there sturdy rails positioned beside all stairs? _____

___ Are there emergency numbers written in large print posted beside each telephone? _____

___ Do you have an emergency exit plan that everyone in the house has rehearsed at least a few times? _____

___ Are there fire extinguishers in the kitchen and on every floor of the house? _____

Additional Items to be Checked:

___ _____ _____

___ _____ _____

___ _____ _____

___ _____ _____

___ _____ _____

___ _____ _____

___ _____ _____

___ _____ _____

___ _____ _____

___ _____ _____

___ _____ _____

___ _____ _____

___ _____ _____

Location of Items at Home

You may know where everything is in the home, but in times of haste or emergency or if a caregiver is helping it is important to have location information documented. Whether looking for a cane, a pair of glasses or the gas shutoff valve, having a comprehensive location guide is not only helpful but can reduce worry and stress in an emergency.

Use the "Location of Items at Home" form that follows to write down the location of basic but important items such as medications, keys, lotion, circuit breakers, gas shutoff valve, lightbulbs and batteries. If you don't wish to note the location of a sensitive item, such as the senior's wallet, note the name and phone numbers of someone who knows where it is.

Location of Items at Home

Basic Everyday Items:

Medications: _____

House Keys: _____

Wallet: _____

Address Book: _____

TV Remote Control: _____

Walking Stick/Cane: _____

Spare Eyeglasses: _____

Lotions, Creams, Personal Care Items: _____

Games/Cards/Checkers: _____

Linens: _____

Underwear:_____

Clothes:_____

First Aid Kit: _____

Other: _____

_____

_____

_____

_____

_____

_____

_____

_____

_____

Location of Items at Home

Other Everyday Items:

Name of Item: _____

Location: _____

Name of Item: _____

Location: _____

Name of Item: _____

Location: _____

Name of Item: _____

Location: _____

Name of Item: _____

Location: _____

Emergency Shutoff Valves/Circuit Breakers

Gas Shutoff Valve: _____

Water Shutoff Valve: _____

Circuit Breakers: _____

Other: _____

_____

_____

_____

_____

Location of Items at Home

Other Emergency Shutoff Items:

Name of Item: _____

Location: _____

Name of Item: _____

Location: _____

Name of Item: _____

Location: _____

Items to Promote Safety

Lightbulbs: _____

Flashlights: _____

Batteries: _____

Fire Extinguisher: _____

Other: _____

_____

_____

_____

_____

_____

_____

_____

_____

_____

Location of Items at Home

Other Items to Promote Safety:

Name of Item: _____

Location: _____

Name of Item: _____

Location: _____

Name of Item: _____

Location: _____

Name of Item: _____

Location: _____

Other: _____

_____

_____

_____

_____

_____

_____

_____

_____

_____

_____

_____

_____

_____

Pet Care Information

If there is a pet in the home it is a good idea to keep contact information for the veterinarian who usually takes care of the animal when it gets sick or needs shots, as well as keeping track of the dates any vaccinations were given. Use the "Pet Care Information" forms that follow to record this data, as well as feeding and other routine or unique care instructions for the animal.

Pet Care Information

Name of Pet: _____

Date of Birth: _____

Favorite Food: _____

_____

Number of Feedings a Day: _____

Exercise Routine (if any): _____

_____

_____

Other Unique Information: _____

_____

_____

Contact Information of Veterinarian

Name: _____

Address: _____

_____

_____

Phone Number: _____

Fax Number: _____

E-mail: _____

Copy this form or download it from *www.biobinders.com/forms*, access code: soforms

Pet Care Information

Pet Medical History

Date: Treatment:

_____   _____

_____   _____

_____   _____

_____   _____

_____   _____

_____   _____

_____   _____

_____   _____

_____   _____

_____   _____

_____   _____

_____   _____

_____   _____

_____   _____

_____   _____

_____   _____

_____   _____

_____   _____

_____   _____

_____   _____

_____   _____

_____   _____

Repair & Maintenance Information

W hen the lights suddenly go out or there's no hot water, you'll want to have it fixed right away! Who are you going to call?

Use the "Repair & Maintenance Information" form that follows to list contact phone numbers for routine and emergency repairs—for example your preferred handyman, electrician, plumber and other workers, the building manager, or another family member.

Copy this form or download it from *www.biobinders.com/forms*, access code: soforms

At Home

Repair & Maintenance Information

Contacts

Handyman

Name: _____

Address: _____

Phone #: _____

Electrician

Name: _____

Address: _____

Phone #: _____

Gardener

Name: _____

Address: _____

Phone #: _____

Other

Name: _____

Address: _____

Phone #: _____

Other

Name: _____

Address: _____

Phone #: _____

Copy this form or download it from *www.biobinders.com/forms*, access code: soforms

Repair & Maintenance Information

Contacts

Other:

Name: _____

Address: _____

Phone #: _____

Other:

Name: _____

Address: _____

Phone #: _____

Other:

Name: _____

Address: _____

Phone #: _____

Other:

Name: _____

Address: _____

Phone #: _____

Other:

Name: _____

Address: _____

Phone #: _____

At Home

Repair & Maintenance Information

Service Date History

Item: _____   Date last serviced: _____

Repairs Performed: _____

Next Service Due: _____

_____

Item: _____   Date last serviced: _____

Repairs Performed: _____

Next Service Due: _____

_____

Item: _____   Date last serviced: _____

Repairs Performed: _____

Next Service Due: _____

_____

Item: _____   Date last serviced: _____

Repairs Performed: _____

Next Service Due: _____

_____

Item: _____   Date last serviced: _____

Repairs Performed: _____

Next Service Due: _____

_____

Item: _____   Date last serviced: _____

Repairs Performed: _____

Next Service Due: _____

Personal Interests

This Personal Interests Section contains the subsections listed below, each of which has its own introduction to help you complete the forms that follow.

Filling out these sections could rekindle some forgotten hobbies or special interests or may be particularly helpful to a caregiver.

- Religious & Personal Customs
- Personal History & Special Interests

Religious & Personal Customs

Religious customs are part of the everyday routine for many people. Perhaps a certain diet must be followed or certain times and places are set aside for daily prayers or other rituals. Going to a church, synagogue, mosque or another house of worship can be a major event that's not to be missed. Even those who aren't "religious"—but who may define themselves as "spiritual," while others may not fall into any definable category—may find significant meaning and pleasure in meditating or just sitting in the garden at a particular time of the day.

Use the "Religious & Personal Customs" form that follows to record the details of these personal, religious or spiritual customs. Recording this information will ensure that a caregiver provides the opportunity to observe these customs, which can help preserve the meaning and beauty in life.

Religious & Personal Customs

Personal History & Special Interests

Back in the 1930s, Betty was a dancer in the Broadway production of *Anything Goes*. During World War II, Bob stormed the beaches on D-Day, having swum ashore after his boat sank. Harriet traveled the country during the war with the Tommy Dorsey orchestra and later became an award-winning photographer.

Most seniors don't volunteer this kind of key information about themselves, so writing it down can be of great help and will enable a caregiver to see the senior as an interesting person who has personal values and great life stories and lessons to share.

Fill out the "Personal History & Special Interests" form that follows, including special talents and hobbies.

Talking about a life's journey can be very illuminating, and you may wish to write in more detail. A senior's life story can be a great gift to pass down to future generations and also help to keep their memories alive.

Personal History & Special Interests

The Senior's Personal History:

_____

_____

_____

_____

_____

_____

_____

_____

_____

_____

_____

_____

Special Talents:

_____

_____

_____

_____

_____

_____

_____

_____

_____

_____

_____

_____

Personal History & Special Interests

Hobbies:

_____
_____
_____
_____
_____
_____
_____
_____
_____
_____
_____
_____
_____

Special Interests:

_____
_____
_____
_____
_____
_____
_____
_____
_____
_____
_____
_____
_____
_____

Personal History & Special Interests

Personal Values:

_____

_____

_____

_____

_____

_____

_____

_____

_____

_____

_____

_____

_____

Life Lessons:

_____

_____

_____

_____

_____

_____

_____

_____

_____

_____

_____

_____

_____

Copy this form or download it from *www.biobinders.com/forms*, access code: soforms

Contacts

The Contacts Section is divided into two sections, which are listed below. Each sub-section has forms to help keep it organized, together with an introductory paragraph.

Should more forms be needed, make photocopies of the pages or download them from *www.biobinders.com.*

- Personal Contacts
- Dates to Remember

Personal Contacts

Use the "Personal Contacts" form that follows to list the contact information of family members, friends or caregivers.

Name: _____

Relationship: _____

Address: _____

_____

_____

Phone: _____

Mobile Phone/Pager: _____

Fax: _____

E-mail: _____

Additional Information: _____

_____

_____

_____

_____

_____

_____

_____

Personal Contacts

Name: _____

Relationship: _____

Address: _____

_____

_____

Phone: _____

Mobile Phone/Pager: _____

Fax: _____

E-mail: _____

Additional Information: _____

_____

_____

_____

_____

_____

_____

_____

_____

Personal Contacts

Name: _____

Relationship: _____

Address: _____

_____

_____

Phone: _____

Mobile Phone/Pager: _____

Fax: _____

E-mail: _____

Additional Information: _____

_____

_____

_____

_____

_____

_____

_____

_____

Copy this form or download it from *www.biobinders.com/forms*, access code: soforms

Personal Contacts

Name: _____

Relationship: _____

Address: _____

_____

_____

Phone: _____

Mobile Phone/Pager: _____

Fax: _____

E-mail: _____

Additional Information: _____

_____

_____

_____

_____

_____

_____

_____

_____

_____

Personal Contacts

Name: _____

Relationship: _____

Address: _____

_____

_____

Phone: _____

Mobile Phone/Pager: _____

Fax: _____

E-mail: _____

Additional Information: _____

_____

_____

_____

_____

_____

_____

_____

_____

_____

_____

_____

Personal Contacts

Name: _____

Relationship: _____

Address: _____

_____

_____

Phone: _____

Mobile Phone/Pager: _____

Fax: _____

E-mail: _____

Additional Information: _____

_____

_____

_____

_____

_____

_____

_____

_____

_____

Dates to Remember

Special occasions are very important to all of us, and they seem to get even more special as we get older. The "Dates to Remember" form will help you keep track of important birthdays, anniversaries, holidays and other occasions. It can also be used to keep a record of gifts given to others, the kinds of things each person likes, and the names of catalogs or stores where gifts might be purchased for that person.

Fill out the "Dates to Remember" forms that follow, adding any pertinent comments.

Dates to Remember

Date	Name of Person	Occasion	Comments
_____	_____	_____	_____
_____	_____	_____	_____
_____	_____	_____	_____
_____	_____	_____	_____
_____	_____	_____	_____
_____	_____	_____	_____
_____	_____	_____	_____
_____	_____	_____	_____
_____	_____	_____	_____
_____	_____	_____	_____
_____	_____	_____	_____
_____	_____	_____	_____
_____	_____	_____	_____
_____	_____	_____	_____
_____	_____	_____	_____
_____	_____	_____	_____
_____	_____	_____	_____
_____	_____	_____	_____
_____	_____	_____	_____
_____	_____	_____	_____
_____	_____	_____	_____
_____	_____	_____	_____
_____	_____	_____	_____
_____	_____	_____	_____
_____	_____	_____	_____
_____	_____	_____	_____

Dates to Remember

Date	Name of Person	Occasion	Comments

Copy this form or download it from *www.biobinders.com/forms*, access code: soforms

Dates to Remember

Date	Name of Person	Occasion	Comments

Dates to Remember

Date	Name of Person	Occasion	Comments

Part II

Legal & Financial

Note: A number of pages in Part Two of this book are labeled with the word "Confidential." This is to bring attention to the fact that the page contains sensitive information that you will want to keep private to protect from identity theft. We recommend you remove, download or copy the page, then complete it and put it in a secure place to safeguard your information.

Legal & Financial Consultants

There are many financial and legal issues that must be handled for a senior. Perhaps you'll need to access financial accounts, make legal decisions, handle real estate transactions and so on. There will undoubtedly be times when you will need to contact the legal and financial advisors who helped to set up documentation to ask questions, access assets, make changes or close accounts.

It is important for a senior to appoint someone to handle his or her financial affairs should he or she become incapacitated, and it is advisable to appoint that person well in advance of the foreseeable need to do so. The Power of Attorney (Financial) document varies from state to state, so it is recommended you consult with an attorney who is licensed to practice law in the state where the principal resides.

Use the "Legal & Financial Consultants" form that follows to write down the names and contact information for the senior's attorney, accountant, stockbroker and other financial and/or legal professionals who can help handle the senior's affairs, and/or who will need to be notified in case of emergency or as needed.

Many CPAs are beginning to offer expertise in "Elder-Care/Prime Plus Services." Check with your own adviser or ask before choosing a new one.

Note: A Power of Attorney for Finances is different from a Durable Power of Attorney for Health. Be sure that the attorney you consult with gives you all the information you might need and that you are fully conversant with the difference.

Legal & Financial Consultants

Attorney

Name: _____

Company: _____

Address: _____

_____

_____

Phone: _____ Fax: _____

E-mail: _____

Matters handled by this attorney: _____

_____

_____

_____

_____

Attorney

Name: _____

Company: _____

Address: _____

_____

_____

Phone: _____ Fax: _____

E-mail: _____

Matters handled by this attorney: _____

_____

_____

_____

Legal & Financial Consultants

Attorney

Name: _____

Company: _____

Address: _____

_____

_____

Phone: _____ Fax: _____

E-mail: _____

Matters handled by this attorney: _____

_____

_____

_____

_____

Accountant/CPA

Name: _____

Company: _____

Address: _____

_____

_____

Phone: _____ Fax: _____

E-mail: _____

Notes: _____

_____

_____

_____

Legal & Financial Consultants

Stockbroker

Name: _____

Company: _____

Address: _____

_____

_____

Phone: _____ Fax: _____

E-mail: _____

Account numbers or location thereof: _____

_____

_____

_____

_____

Stockbroker

Name: _____

Company: _____

Address: _____

_____

_____

Phone: _____ Fax: _____

E-mail: _____

Account numbers or location thereof: _____

_____

_____

_____

Legal & Financial Consultants

Stockbroker

Name: _____

Company: _____

Address: _____

_____

_____

Phone: _____ Fax: _____

E-mail: _____

Account numbers or location thereof: _____

_____

_____

_____

_____

Insurance Broker

Name: _____

Company: _____

Address: _____

_____

_____

Phone: _____ Fax: _____

E-mail: _____

Account numbers or location thereof: _____

_____

_____

_____

Legal & Financial Consultants

Other Legal or Financial Consultant

Name: _____

Company: _____

Address: _____

_____

_____

Phone: _____   Fax: _____

E-mail: _____

Account numbers or location thereof: _____

_____

_____

_____

_____

Other Legal or Financial Consultant

Name: _____

Company: _____

Address: _____

_____

_____

Phone: _____   Fax: _____

E-mail: _____

Account numbers or location thereof: _____

_____

_____

_____

Power of Attorney (Financial)

To avoid any problems with a Financial Power of Attorney the senior should contact all financial institutions where he or she has accounts as soon as the document is executed, providing them with a copy. At the same time, other authorizations or signature cards required by a particular institution should be executed. It is also important to keep a record of the contact information for the attorney who authored the document.

If you are in any doubt about the nature of this document please refer to the information at the beginning of the Legal & Financial Section or go to the AARP Web site at *www.aarp.org*.

Name of Attorney-in-fact: _____

Relationship to senior (if any): _____

Address: _____

_____

Phone: _____ Fax: _____

E-mail: _____

Notes: _____

_____

Name of Attorney: _____

Relationship to senior (if any): _____

Address: _____

_____

Phone: _____ Fax: _____

E-mail: _____

Notes: _____

_____

Note: A Power of Attorney for Finances is different from a Durable Power of Attorney for Health. Be sure that you are fully conversant with the difference.

Probate

Attorneys/Mediators Involved:

_____

_____

_____

_____

_____

Consultants/CPAs Involved:

_____

_____

_____

_____

Interested Parties Involved:

_____

_____

_____

_____

_____

Pending Issues:

_____

_____

_____

_____

_____

_____

_____

Settlements

Attorneys/Mediators Involved:

_____
_____
_____
_____
_____

Consultants/CPAs Involved:

_____
_____
_____
_____

Interested Parties Involved:

_____
_____
_____
_____

Pending Issues:

_____
_____
_____
_____
_____
_____

Pending Legal Issues

Lawsuits

Attorneys/Mediators Involved:

_____

_____

_____

_____

_____

Consultants/CPAs Involved:

_____

_____

_____

_____

_____

Interested Parties Involved:

_____

_____

_____

_____

_____

Pending Issues:

_____

_____

_____

_____

_____

_____

Pending Legal Issues

Divorce

Attorneys/Mediators Involved:

_____

_____

_____

_____

_____

Consultants/CPAs Involved:

_____

_____

_____

_____

Interested Parties Involved:

_____

_____

_____

_____

Pending Issues:

_____

_____

_____

_____

_____

_____

Personal & Family Legal Documents

Birth certificates, marital documents and powers of attorney are just a few of the documents that can be needed to handle matters from the routine to the extraordinary. Unfortunately these documents are often kept in more than one place, and locating them can be difficult, especially if they are not well organized.

Use the "Personal & Family Legal Documents" form that follows to record the locations of key personal and family legal documents or write in the name and phone number of who would have them.

Indicate below where the documents are located or who should be contacted.

Adoption Papers: _____

_____

_____

Birth Certificate: _____

_____

_____

Citizenship Papers: _____

_____

_____

Resident Papers: _____

_____

_____

Durable Power of Attorney for Health Care: _____

_____

_____

Power of Attorney (Financial): _____

_____

_____

Guardianship/Conservator Paperwork: _____

_____

_____

Military Discharge Papers: _____

_____

_____

Passport: _____

_____

_____

Marital/Family

Indicate below where the documents are located or who should be contacted.

Marriage Certificate:

_____

_____

_____

Divorce/Separation Papers (if any): _____

_____

_____

_____

Prenuptial/Postnuptial Agreement: _____

_____

_____

_____

Adoption Papers (children's): _____

_____

_____

_____

Birth Certificate (children's): _____

_____

_____

_____

Death Certificate of Spouse: _____

_____

_____

_____

Other: _____

_____

_____

_____

_____

_____

_____

_____

_____

_____

_____

_____

_____

_____

_____

_____

_____

_____

_____

_____

_____

_____

_____

_____

_____

_____

_____

_____

_____

_____

_____

_____

_____

Replacing Vital Documents

Birth Certificate:

Where to Get a New One:

Start with the Vital Statistics Office in the birth state. (Do not call the hospital where the birth took place.) Check the government pages of the phone book to get the phone number and address of the National Center for Health Statistics office in your state, or go to their Web site to get what you need at *www.cdc.gov/nchs.*

What You Need to Get It:

Collect as many vital statistics as you can: name, gender, parents' names, place of birth and date of birth, or as much information as possible. Some states also require a photo ID. Check for current fees.

How Long It Takes:

If you go in person you might be able to walk away with your replacement. If you apply by mail you could wait up to four weeks, or possibly two if you pay an expedite fee. Some states may offer an overnight service. During the late summer processing could take longer as parents request birth certificates for children beginning school.

Social Security Card:

Where to Get a New One:

In person at your local Social Security office, check the government pages of the phone book or check on their Web site at *www.socialsecurity.gov.* (There are approximately 1,300 offices across the nation.) You can download an application from the site. Social Security Administration warns against mailing a request with the supporting documents, citing stolen mail and identity theft as a huge problem.

What You Need to Get It:

After completing the one-page application it should be accompanied by one original identifying document (photocopies are not acceptable), such as your driver's license, passport, marriage or divorce documents. There is no charge for a replacement. If born outside the U.S., you may need to show proof of citizenship or lawful alien status.

How Long It Takes:

If you go in person to the Social Security office it could take as little as five minutes to process your request, and your new card will be mailed within two weeks. The Social Security Administration can give you a printout on its letterhead that verifies your number to use in the meantime.

Personal & Family Legal Documents

Replacing Vital Documents

Passport:

<u>Where to Get a New One:</u>
If you have lost or had your passport stolen, you must appear in person at a passport processing facility to request a replacement. You can call 877-487-2778 to obtain order forms and instructions, or go to the U.S. Department of State's Web site, *www.travel.state.gov,* for a list of office locations, plus forms and instructions.

<u>What You Need to Get It:</u>
After completing the application for a replacement passport you will need proof of U.S. citizenship (such as a birth certificate), proof of identify and two passport photos. The Web site has information about additional requirements for expedited requests.

<u>How Long It Takes:</u>
Regular service is approximately six weeks. Expedited service is an additional cost but you will receive your passport in approximately two weeks. Check for current fees. Check online or in your local phone directory for a nongovernmental expediting service. Their charges will vary, but they are reliable and can get your replacement in one to three days.

Old Tax Returns

<u>Where to Get a New One:</u>
Your tax preparer or accountant will usually keep copies of your returns on file; however you can also get copies of federal returns directly from the Internal Revenue Service. Call **800-829-1040** to get the necessary forms, or visit *www.irs.gov* to download them.

<u>What You Need to Get It:</u>
A completed IRS Form 4506 together with the current fee payable for each duplicate return requested.

<u>How Long It Takes:</u>
It can take up to sixty days to receive copies of your requested returns.

Personal & Family Legal Documents

Replacing Vital Documents

Car Title:

Where to Get a New One:
You can get an application for a replacement title from the Department of Motor Vehicles. Check for locations in the government pages in your local phone book.

What You Need to Get It:
You will need to show identification and proof of ownership of the car such as vehicle registration, your vehicle identification number or your license-plate number. Complete the DMV application, and submit it together with the fee, which varies from state to state.

How Long It Takes:
You could receive the replacement as quickly as four days, but again, it varies from state to state.

Property Deed:

Where to Get a New One:
Check with the lawyer who handled your closing. After the county records your deed, the copy is either returned to you or your attorney. If your attorney does not have it you should call the county clerk's office. You could also look in the Yellow Pages under "Title Search" for a title company, and hire them to do a search for you.

What You Need to Get It:
The street address of the property together with the tax map ID number will expedite the process. No fee is charged if you request the title yourself, although the city may charge copying fees. If you decide to use a title company, be sure to ask what they will charge to do the research for you.

How Long It Takes:
It takes approximately ten business days.

Bank/Financial Institution Accounts

Many people have multiple accounts at banks, credit unions and/or brokerages, and it's easy to forget about them if a comprehensive list isn't kept.

Use the "Bank/Financial Institution Accounts" form that follows to write down the contact information for all financial institutions where accounts are located, along with account numbers and safe deposit box numbers (if any), or write down the name and phone number of who would have this information.

Bank Accounts

Name of Bank/Financial Institution: _____

_____

Address: _____

_____

_____

Phone: _____   Fax: _____

Web site: _____

Account number or location thereof:

Checking: _____

Password/Pin # or Clue for Internet or phone access: _____

Savings: _____

Password/Pin # or Clue for Internet or phone access: _____

C.D.: _____

Other: _____

_____

_____

Safe Deposit Box #: _____   Location of keys: _____

_____

_____

_____

_____

_____

Bank Accounts

Name of Bank/Financial Institution: _____

_____

Address: _____

_____

_____

Phone: _____ Fax: _____

Web site: _____

<u>Account number or location thereof:</u>

Checking: _____

Password/Pin # or Clue for Internet or phone access: _____

Savings: _____

Password/Pin # or Clue for Internet or phone access: _____

C.D.: _____

Other: _____

_____

_____

Safe Deposit Box #: _____ Location of keys: _____

_____

_____

_____

_____

_____

Other Financial Institution Accounts

Name of Bank/Financial Institution: _____

_____

Address: _____

_____

_____

Phone: _____ Fax: _____

Web site: _____

Account number or location thereof:

Checking: _____

Password/Pin # or Clue for Internet or phone access: _____

Savings: _____

Password/Pin # or Clue for Internet or phone access: _____

C.D.: _____

Other: _____

_____

_____

Safe Deposit Box #: _____ Location of keys: _____

_____

_____

_____

_____

_____

Other Financial Institution Accounts

Name of Bank/Financial Institution: _____

_____

Address: _____

_____

_____

Phone: _____   Fax: _____

Web site: _____

Account number or location thereof:

Checking: _____

Password/Pin # or Clue for Internet or phone access: _____

Savings: _____

Password/Pin # or Clue for Internet or phone access: _____

C.D.: _____

Other: _____

_____

_____

Safe Deposit Box #: _____   Location of keys: _____

_____

_____

_____

_____

_____

Copy this form or download it from *www.biobinders.com/forms*, access code: soforms

Credit Cards/Charge Accounts

Many people have ten or more credit cards and charge accounts, and don't keep a detailed record of them all.

Use the "Credit Cards/Charge Accounts" form that follows to write down the names, account numbers, contact information in case of loss or theft and any other important details for all credit cards, charge or debit accounts, or any other accounts.

Credit Cards

Credit Card: Type of card (i.e., Visa, MasterCard, etc.) _____

_____

Account #: _____

_____

Password/Pin # or Clue for Internet or phone access: _____

Customer Service Address: _____

_____

_____

_____

Phone: _____   Fax: _____

Web site: _____

Credit Card: Type of card (i.e., Visa, MasterCard, etc.) _____

_____

Account #: _____

_____

Password/Pin # or Clue for Internet or phone access: _____

Customer Service Address: _____

_____

_____

_____

Phone: _____   Fax: _____

Web site: _____

Credit Cards

Credit Card: Type of card (i.e., Visa, MasterCard, etc.) _____

_____

Account #: _____

_____

Password/Pin # or Clue for Internet or phone access: _____

Customer Service Address: _____

_____

_____

_____

Phone: _____   Fax: _____

Web site: _____

Credit Card: Type of card (i.e., Visa, MasterCard, etc.) _____

_____

Account #: _____

_____

Password/Pin # or Clue for Internet or phone access: _____

Customer Service Address: _____

_____

_____

_____

Phone: _____   Fax: _____

Web site: _____

Charge Accounts

Charge Account: Type of card (i.e., department store, gasoline, etc.) _____

Account #: _____

Password/Pin # or Clue for Internet or phone access: _____

Customer Service Address: _____

_____

_____

Phone: _____ Fax: _____

Web site: _____

Charge Account: Type of card (i.e., department store, gasoline, etc.) _____

Account #: _____

Password/Pin # or Clue for Internet or phone access: _____

Customer Service Address: _____

_____

_____

Phone: _____ Fax: _____

Web site: _____

Charge Accounts

Charge Account: Type of card (i.e., department store, gasoline, etc.) _____

_____

Account #: _____

_____

Password/Pin # or Clue for Internet or phone access: _____

Customer Service Address: _____

_____

_____

_____

Phone: _____   Fax: _____

Web site: _____

Charge Account: Type of card (i.e., department store, gasoline, etc.) _____

_____

Account #: _____

_____

Password/Pin # or Clue for Internet or phone access: _____

Customer Service Address: _____

_____

_____

_____

Phone: _____   Fax: _____

Web site: _____

Debit Accounts

Debit Account Name: _____

Account #: _____

Password/Pin # or Clue for Internet or phone access: _____

_____

Customer Service Address: _____

Phone: _____   Fax: _____

Web site: _____

Debit Account Name: _____

Account #: _____

Password/Pin # or Clue for Internet or phone access: _____

_____

Customer Service Address: _____

Phone: _____   Fax: _____

Web site: _____

Debit Account Name: _____

Account #: _____

Password/Pin # or Clue for Internet or phone access: _____

_____

Customer Service Address: _____

Phone: _____   Fax: _____

Web site: _____

Debit Accounts

Debit Account Name: _____

Account #: _____

Password/Pin # or Clue for Internet or phone access: _____

_____

Customer Service Address: _____

Phone: _____   Fax: _____

Web site: _____

Debit Account Name: _____

Account #: _____

Password/Pin # or Clue for Internet or phone access: _____

_____

Customer Service Address: _____

Phone: _____   Fax: _____

Web site: _____

Debit Account Name: _____

Account #: _____

Password/Pin # or Clue for Internet or phone access: _____

_____

Customer Service Address: _____

Phone: _____   Fax: _____

Web site: _____

Other Accounts

Financial Investments Information

It can be difficult to keep track of all the stocks, bonds, mutual funds, annuities, 401(k)s, CDs and other investments that one accumulates throughout a lifetime, especially since accounts can be set up through work, banks, insurance companies, brokerages or online. That's why it's important to list them all, plus contact information.

Use the "Financial Investments Information" form that follows to write down the names and contact information for the brokerages and other institutions that handle all financial investments. Also, list the name and contact information for the person who has been given Financial Power of Attorney (if any).

Stocks

Name of Financial Institution: _____

_____

Contact Person for this account: _____

Address: _____

_____

_____

Phone: _____   Fax: _____

E-mail: _____

Web site: _____

Password/Pin # or Clue for Internet or phone access: _____

_____

_____

Account numbers or location thereof: _____

_____

_____

Paperwork location/who to contact: _____

_____

_____

_____

Appointed Power of Attorney (if any): _____

_____

_____

_____

_____

_____

Stocks

Name of Financial Institution: _____

_____

Contact Person for this account: _____

Address: _____

_____

_____

Phone: _____   Fax: _____

E-mail: _____

Web site: _____

Password/Pin # or Clue for Internet or phone access: _____

_____

_____

Account numbers or location thereof: _____

_____

_____

Paperwork location/who to contact: _____

_____

_____

_____

Appointed Power of Attorney (if any): _____

_____

_____

_____

_____

Bonds

Name of Financial Institution: _____

_____

Contact Person for this account: _____

Address: _____

_____

_____

Phone: _____   Fax: _____

E-mail: _____

Web site: _____

Password/Pin # or Clue for Internet or phone access: _____

_____

_____

Account numbers or location thereof: _____

_____

_____

Paperwork location/who to contact: _____

_____

_____

_____

Appointed Power of Attorney (if any): _____

_____

_____

_____

_____

_____

Bonds

Name of Financial Institution: _____

_____

Contact Person for this account: _____

Address: _____

_____

_____

Phone: _____   Fax: _____

E-mail: _____

Web site:_____

Password/Pin # or Clue for Internet or phone access: _____

_____

_____

Account numbers or location thereof: _____

_____

_____

Paperwork location/who to contact: _____

_____

_____

_____

Appointed Power of Attorney (if any): _____

_____

_____

_____

_____

Mutual Funds

Name of Financial Institution: _____

_____

Contact Person for this account: _____

Address: _____

_____

_____

Phone: _____ Fax: _____

E-mail: _____

Web site: _____

Password/Pin # or Clue for Internet or phone access: _____

_____

_____

Account numbers or location thereof: _____

_____

_____

Paperwork location/who to contact: _____

_____

_____

_____

Appointed Power of Attorney (if any): _____

_____

_____

_____

_____

_____

Mutual Funds

Name of Financial Institution: _____

_____

Contact Person for this account: _____

Address: _____

_____

_____

Phone: _____   Fax: _____

E-mail: _____

Web site: _____

Password/Pin # or Clue for Internet or phone access: _____

_____

_____

Account numbers or location thereof: _____

_____

_____

Paperwork location/who to contact: _____

_____

_____

_____

Appointed Power of Attorney (if any): _____

_____

_____

_____

_____

_____

Annuities

Name of Financial Institution: _____

_____

Contact Person for this account: _____

Address: _____

_____

_____

Phone: _____   Fax: _____

E-mail: _____

Web site: _____

Password/Pin # or Clue for Internet or phone access: _____

_____

_____

Account numbers or location thereof: _____

_____

_____

Paperwork location/who to contact: _____

_____

_____

_____

Appointed Power of Attorney (if any): _____

_____

_____

_____

_____

_____

Annuities

Name of Financial Institution: _____

_____

Contact Person for this account: _____

Address: _____

_____

_____

Phone: _____   Fax: _____

E-mail: _____

Web site: _____

Password/Pin # or Clue for Internet or phone access: _____

_____

_____

Account numbers or location thereof: _____

_____

_____

Paperwork location/who to contact: _____

_____

_____

_____

Appointed Power of Attorney (if any): _____

_____

_____

_____

_____

_____

Name of Financial Institution: _____

_____

Contact Person for this account: _____

Address: _____

_____

_____

Phone: _____   Fax: _____

E-mail: _____

Web site: _____

Password/Pin # or Clue for Internet or phone access: _____

_____

_____

Account numbers or location thereof: _____

_____

_____

Paperwork location/who to contact: _____

_____

_____

_____

Appointed Power of Attorney (if any): _____

_____

_____

_____

_____

_____

CDs

Name of Financial Institution: _____

_____

Contact Person for this account: _____

Address: _____

_____

_____

Phone: _____   Fax: _____

E-mail: _____

Web site: _____

Password/Pin # or Clue for Internet or phone access: _____

_____

_____

Account numbers or location thereof: _____

_____

_____

Paperwork location/who to contact: _____

_____

_____

_____

Appointed Power of Attorney (if any): _____

_____

_____

_____

_____

_____

401(k)s

Name of Financial Institution: _____

_____

Contact Person for this account: _____

Address: _____

_____

_____

Phone: _____   Fax: _____

E-mail: _____

Web site: _____

Password/Pin # or Clue for Internet or phone access: _____

_____

_____

Account numbers or location thereof: _____

_____

_____

Paperwork location/who to contact: _____

_____

_____

_____

Appointed Power of Attorney (if any): _____

_____

_____

_____

_____

_____

401(k)s

Name of Financial Institution: _____

_____

Contact Person for this account: _____

Address: _____

_____

_____

Phone: _____   Fax: _____

E-mail: _____

Web site:_____

Password/Pin # or Clue for Internet or phone access: _____

_____

_____

Account numbers or location thereof: _____

_____

_____

Paperwork location/who to contact: _____

_____

_____

_____

Appointed Power of Attorney (if any): _____

_____

_____

_____

_____

_____

Other Financial Investments

Name of Financial Institution: _____

_____

Contact Person for this account: _____

Address: _____

_____

_____

Phone: _____ Fax: _____

E-mail: _____

Web site: _____

Password/Pin # or Clue for Internet or phone access: _____

_____

_____

Account numbers or location thereof: _____

_____

_____

Paperwork location/who to contact: _____

_____

_____

_____

Appointed Power of Attorney (if any): _____

_____

_____

_____

_____

_____

Other Financial Investments

Name of Financial Institution: _____

_____

Contact Person for this account: _____

Address: _____

_____

_____

Phone: _____   Fax: _____

E-mail: _____

Web site:_____

Password/Pin # or Clue for Internet or phone access: _____

_____

_____

Account numbers or location thereof: _____

_____

_____

Paperwork location/who to contact: _____

_____

_____

_____

Appointed Power of Attorney (if any): _____

_____

_____

_____

_____

_____

Other Financial Information

After a lifetime of working, purchasing homes and businesses, borrowing and lending money, a senior may have accumulated many miscellaneous assets and/or liabilities.

Use the "Other Financial Information" form that follows to write down the location of information regarding loans, mortgages, promissory notes and other financial interests, or the name and phone number of who has this information.

Assets

Business Interests/Ownership Information

Name of business: _____

Location of documents: _____

_____

Name of business: _____

Location of documents: _____

_____

Name of business: _____

Location of documents: _____

_____

Name of business: _____

Location of documents: _____

_____

Name of business: _____

Location of documents: _____

_____

Name of business: _____

Location of documents: _____

_____

Name of business: _____

Location of documents: _____

_____

Name of business: _____

Location of documents: _____

_____

Name of business: _____

Location of documents: _____

_____

Assets

Business Interests/Ownership Information

Name of business: _____

Location of documents: _____

_____

Name of business: _____

Location of documents: _____

_____

Name of business: _____

Location of documents: _____

_____

Name of business: _____

Location of documents: _____

_____

Name of business: _____

Location of documents: _____

_____

Name of business: _____

Location of documents: _____

_____

Name of business: _____

Location of documents: _____

_____

Name of business: _____

Location of documents: _____

_____

Name of business: _____

Location of documents: _____

_____

Liabilities

Outstanding Loans

Name of business: _____

Location of documents: _____

_____

Name of business: _____

Location of documents: _____

_____

Name of business: _____

Location of documents: _____

_____

Name of business: _____

Location of documents: _____

_____

Name of business: _____

Location of documents: _____

_____

Name of business: _____

Location of documents: _____

_____

Name of business: _____

Location of documents: _____

_____

Name of business: _____

Location of documents: _____

_____

Name of business: _____

Location of documents: _____

_____

Liabilities

Outstanding Loans

Name of business: _____

Location of documents: _____

_____

Name of business: _____

Location of documents: _____

_____

Name of business: _____

Location of documents: _____

_____

Name of business: _____

Location of documents: _____

_____

Name of business: _____

Location of documents: _____

_____

Name of business: _____

Location of documents: _____

_____

Name of business: _____

Location of documents: _____

_____

Name of business: _____

Location of documents: _____

_____

Name of business: _____

Location of documents: _____

_____

Tax Information

Questions can sometimes arise after taxes have been filed; also, disability or other life changes can have important tax consequences. It is recommended to save at least three years' past tax returns and advisable to keep a record of your tax preparer's contact information.

Use the "Tax Information" forms that follow to write down the location of both past and current tax information.

Income Tax Returns

Year of Tax Return: _____

Name of Tax Preparer: _____

_____

Location of documents or who to contact: _____

_____

_____

_____

Year of Tax Return: _____

Name of Tax Preparer: _____

_____

Location of documents or who to contact: _____

_____

_____

_____

Year of Tax Return: _____

Name of Tax Preparer: _____

_____

Location of documents or who to contact: _____

_____

_____

_____

Copy this form or download it from *www.biobinders.com/forms*, access code: soforms

Current Tax Information & Receipts

It is a good idea to keep all tax-related documentation in one place. Keep track of any home improvement records, medical expenses, donations to charities, year-end statements and other receipts. Your tax preparer will let you know what is not applicable.

Location of documents or who to contact: _____

_____

_____

_____

_____

_____

_____

_____

_____

_____

Property Tax Bills & Receipts

In addition to keeping all property tax bills and receipts, you may want to save any appraisals.

Address of Property:

_____

_____

Location of documents or who to contact:

_____

_____

Address of Property:

_____

_____

Location of documents or who to contact:

_____

_____

Address of Property:

_____

_____

Location of documents or who to contact:

_____

_____

Copy this form or download it from *www.biobinders.com/forms*, access code: soforms

Other Tax Information

Other Tax Information

Location of documents or who to contact:

_____

_____

_____

_____

_____

_____

Other Tax Information

Location of documents or who to contact:

_____

_____

_____

_____

_____

_____

Other Tax Information

Location of documents or who to contact:

_____

_____

_____

_____

_____

_____

Real Estate

Mortgage payments, leases, co-ownership property agreements, property taxes, and insurance and real estate documents must be monitored to make sure payments are made and received on time.

Use the "Real Estate Information" form that follows to write down the location of information regarding home(s) and/or other real estate.

Address of Property:

_____

_____

Location of documents or who to contact:

_____

_____

Date Purchased: _____ Date Sold: _____

Address of Property:

_____

_____

Location of documents or who to contact:

_____

_____

Date Purchased: _____ Date Sold: _____

Address of Property:

_____

_____

Location of documents or who to contact:

_____

_____

Date Purchased: _____ Date Sold: _____

Co-ownership Property Agreements

Address of Property:

_____

_____

Location of documents or who to contact:

_____

_____

Date Purchased: _____ Date Sold: _____

Address of Property:

_____

_____

Location of documents or who to contact:

_____

_____

Date Purchased: _____ Date Sold: _____

Address of Property: _____

_____

Names of Co-Owners _____

_____

Location of documents or who to contact: _____

_____

Date Purchased: _____ Date Sold: _____

Mortgages

Address of Property: _____

_____

Date and Length of Loan: _____

Name of Lender: _____

_____

Location of documents or who to contact: _____

_____

Address of Property: _____

_____

Date and Length of Loan: _____

Name of Lender: _____

_____

Location of documents or who to contact: _____

_____

Address of Property: _____

_____

Date and Length of Loan: _____

Name of Lender: _____

_____

Location of documents or who to contact: _____

_____

Address of Property: _____

_____

Name of Tenant: _____

_____

Date and Length of Lease: _____

Location of documents or who to contact: _____

_____

Address of Property: _____

_____

Name of Tenant: _____

_____

Date and Length of Lease: _____

Location of documents or who to contact: _____

_____

Address of Property: _____

_____

Name of Tenant: _____

_____

Date and Length of Lease: _____

Location of documents or who to contact: _____

_____

Appraisals

Address of Property: _____

_____

Location of documents or who to contact: _____

_____

Date Appraised: _____Value: _____
Appraiser: _____

_____

Address of Property: _____

_____

Location of documents or who to contact: _____

_____

Date Appraised: _____Value: _____
Appraiser: _____

_____

Address of Property: _____

_____

Location of documents or who to contact: _____

_____

Date Appraised: _____Value: _____
Appraiser: _____

_____

Other Property Documents

Name of Document/Property: _____

_____

Location of documents or who to contact: _____

_____

Additional Information:_____

_____

_____

Name of Document/Property: _____

_____

Location of documents or who to contact: _____

_____

Additional Information:_____

_____

_____

Name of Document/Property: _____

_____

Location of documents or who to contact: _____

_____

Additional Information:_____

_____

_____

Personal Property

Jewelry, art and other personal property can be of great sentimental value and may also have great financial value. For these reasons, it's important to know the location of all personal property, as well as documents relating to appraisals and other matters.

Use the "Personal Property Information" form that follows to write down the location of information regarding personal property or the name and phone number of who has this information.

Vehicles

Vehicle Title (pink slip)

Make and Model of vehicle: _____

_____

Date of Purchase/Loan: _____

_____

Dealership/Seller: _____

_____

Date Sold/Purchaser: _____

_____

Location of document or who to contact: _____

_____

Vehicle Registration

Make and Model of vehicle: _____

_____

Location of document or who to contact: _____

_____

Vehicle Repair Records

Make and Model of vehicle: _____

Location of documents or who to contact: _____

_____

Date Warranty Expires (if any): _____

_____

Vehicles

Vehicle Title (pink slip)

Make and Model of vehicle: _____

_____

Date of Purchase/Loan: _____

_____

Dealership/Seller: _____

_____

Date Sold/Purchaser: _____

_____

Location of document or who to contact: _____

_____

Vehicle Registration

Make and Model of vehicle: _____

_____

Location of document or who to contact: _____

_____

Vehicle Repair Records

Make and Model of vehicle: _____

Location of documents or who to contact: _____

_____

Date Warranty Expires (if any): _____

_____

Jewelry

Name of piece: _____

Location: _____

Location of appraisal (if any): _____

Name of piece: _____

Location: _____

Location of appraisal (if any): _____

Name of piece: _____

Location: _____

Location of appraisal (if any): _____

Name of piece: _____

Location: _____

Location of appraisal (if any): _____

Name of piece: _____

Location: _____

Location of appraisal (if any): _____

Name of piece: _____

Location: _____

Location of appraisal (if any): _____

Name of piece: _____

Location: _____

Location of appraisal (if any): _____

Art and Furniture

Name of piece: _____

Location: _____

Location of appraisal (if any): _____

Name of piece: _____

Location: _____

Location of appraisal (if any): _____

Name of piece: _____

Location: _____

Location of appraisal (if any): _____

Name of piece: _____

Location: _____

Location of appraisal (if any): _____

Name of piece: _____

Location: _____

Location of appraisal (if any): _____

Name of piece: _____

Location: _____

Location of appraisal (if any): _____

Name of piece: _____

Location: _____

Location of appraisal (if any): _____

Other Valuable/ Personal Property

Name of piece: _____

Location: _____

Location of appraisal (if any): _____

Name of piece: _____

Location: _____

Location of appraisal (if any): _____

Name of piece: _____

Location: _____

Location of appraisal (if any): _____

Name of piece: _____

Location: _____

Location of appraisal (if any): _____

Name of piece: _____

Location: _____

Location of appraisal (if any): _____

Name of piece: _____

Location: _____

Location of appraisal (if any): _____

Name of piece: _____

Location: _____

Location of appraisal (if any): _____

Insurance Information

It's vital to know which insurance policies have been taken out, what they offer and what must be done to keep them current, as well as updating the names of beneficiaries should they change.

Use the "Insurance Information" form that follows to write down the names of the companies issuing the various insurance accounts, their contact information, the account numbers and other pertinent information. Noting the location of a medical insurance benefit booklet could also be very helpful for a caregiver or family member.

Life Insurance

Life Insurance

Name of Company: _____

Contact: _____

Address: _____

_____

Phone: _____ Fax: _____

E-mail: _____

Account #: _____

Location of document or insurance card and policy: _____

_____

_____

_____

Life Insurance

Name of Company: _____

Contact: _____

Address: _____

_____

Phone: _____ Fax: _____

E-mail: _____

Account #: _____

Location of document or insurance card and policy: _____

_____

_____

_____

Auto Insurance

Auto Insurance (First Auto)

Make/Year: _____ Model:_____

Color: _____

Name of Company: _____

Contact: _____

Address: _____

_____

Phone: _____ Fax: _____

E-mail: _____

Account #: _____

Location of document or insurance card and policy: _____

_____

_____

Auto Insurance (Second Auto)

Make/Year: _____ Model:_____

Color: _____

Name of Company: _____

Contact: _____

Address: _____

_____

Phone: _____ Fax: _____

E-mail: _____

Account #: _____

Location of document or insurance card and policy: _____

_____

_____

Property Insurance

Home Owners/Renter's Insurance

Name of Company: _____

Contact: _____

Address: _____

_____

Phone: _____   Fax: _____

E-mail: _____

Account #: _____

Location of document or insurance card and policy: _____

_____

_____

_____

Home Warranty Insurance

Name of Company: _____

Contact: _____

Address: _____

_____

Phone: _____   Fax: _____

E-mail: _____

Account #: _____

Location of document or insurance card and policy: _____

_____

_____

_____

Liability & Fire Insurance

Liability Insurance

Name of Company: _____

Contact: _____

Address: _____

_____

Phone: _____   Fax: _____

E-mail: _____

Account #: _____

Location of document or insurance card and policy: _____

_____

_____

_____

Fire Insurance

Name of Company: _____

Contact: _____

Address: _____

_____

Phone: _____   Fax: _____

E-mail: _____

Account #: _____

Location of document or insurance card and policy: _____

_____

_____

_____

Insurance

Disability & Long-Term Care Insurance

Disability Insurance

Name of Company: _____

Contact: _____

Address: _____

_____

Phone: _____ Fax: _____

E-mail: _____

Account #: _____

Location of document or insurance card and policy: _____

_____

_____

_____

Long-Term Care Insurance

Name of Company: _____

Contact: _____

Address: _____

_____

Phone: _____ Fax: _____

E-mail: _____

Account #: _____

Location of document or insurance card and policy: _____

_____

_____

_____

Other Insurance

Other Insurance

Type of Insurance: _____

Name of Company: _____

Contact: _____

Address: _____

_____

Phone: _____   Fax: _____

E-mail: _____

Account #: _____

Location of document or insurance card and policy: _____

_____

_____

_____

Other Insurance

Type of Insurance: _____

Name of Company: _____

Contact: _____

Address: _____

_____

Phone: _____   Fax: _____

E-mail: _____

Account #: _____

Location of document or insurance card and policy: _____

_____

_____

_____

Retirement Benefits

In later life a senior's financial stability will most likely depend on Social Security and other retirement benefits. Therefore, it's vital to know how much money can be expected every month and what, if anything, must be done to keep the benefits coming.

Use the "Retirement Benefits Information" form that follows to write down the location of information about Social Security, retirement benefits, and benefits from other organizations, or the name and phone number of who has this information.

Social Security Benefits

Social Security ID # _____

Location of Social Security Card: _____

_____

_____

_____

_____

_____

Location of Social Security Statements: _____

_____

_____

_____

Pension Information

Pension Information

Name of Company: _____

Contact: _____

Address: _____

_____

Phone: _____ Fax: _____

E-mail: _____

Account #: _____

Location of document or insurance card and policy: _____

_____

_____

_____

Pension Information

Name of Company: _____

Contact: _____

Address: _____

_____

Phone: _____ Fax: _____

E-mail: _____

Account #: _____

Location of document or insurance card and policy: _____

_____

_____

_____

Other Benefits

Other Information

Name of Company: _____

Contact: _____

Address: _____

_____

Phone: _____   Fax: _____

E-mail: _____

Account #: _____

Location of document or insurance card and policy: _____

_____

_____

_____

Other Information

Name of Company: _____

Contact: _____

Address: _____

_____

Phone: _____   Fax: _____

E-mail: _____

Account #: _____

Location of document or insurance card and policy: _____

_____

_____

_____

Health Directives Durable Power of Attorney for Health

An advance directive, typically referred to as a "Durable Power of Attorney for Health Care" or "Living Will," is a document that lets the senior give instructions about his or her future health care. It also allows for the appointment of someone to make health care decisions when a senior is no longer able to make them.

A DNR or "Do Not Resuscitate" instruction can be included in the Durable Power of Attorney for Health Care or Living Will. It is a directive that will give clear instructions to a medical emergency team, should the senior's heart stop beating, about his or her wishes regarding the use of CPR or cardiopulmonary resuscitation.

Laws vary from one state to another. Most states have their own "Living Will" forms; alternatively a senior could write out his or her own preferences regarding medical treatment. A "Durable Power of Attorney for Health Care" is a signed, dated and witnessed document that names an "agent" and can include instructions about specific medical treatment that may or may not be desired by the senior. Laws in some states may make it preferable to have one rather than the other; it may be possible to have both or even combine them into a single document. Seek advice from both a doctor and an attorney about the circumstances around which an advance directive will be used and the differing formats and laws from state to state.

Signed copies of either document should be on file with health providers, the current acting attorney and family members. Since the laws vary from state to state, see an attorney about the proper procedure for your state.

Use the "Health Directives Information" form that follows to write down the location of the Durable Power or Attorney for Health Care or the Living Will.

Durable Power of Attorney or Living Will

Durable Power of Attorney

Location of document or who to contact: _____

_____

_____

_____

Date executed: _____

Living Will

Location of document or who to contact: _____

_____

_____

_____

Date executed: _____

Other information: _____

_____

_____

_____

_____

_____

End of Life

Emotions run high when a senior's life draws to a close. While it can be difficult to think about these issues now, it's best to put the paperwork in order in advance as that will make it much easier for other family members to take care of all the necessary arrangements.

Use the "End of Life Information" form that follows to write down the location of a will, trust, funeral arrangements, eulogy, any other special instructions and cemetery plot.

Will and Eulogy

Will/Last Will & Testament

Location of document: _____

_____

_____

_____

_____

Date executed: _____

Eulogy

Location of document or who to contact: _____

_____

_____

_____

_____

Trust Information

Type of Trust: _____

_____

Name of Trust: _____

_____

Date Executed: _____

_____

Primary Beneficiary: _____

_____

Contingent Beneficiary: _____

_____

Primary Trustee: _____

_____

Successor Trustee: _____

_____

Location of Document: _____

_____

_____

Funeral/Cemetery Information

Funeral Arrangements/Instructions:

Location of document or who to contact: _____

_____

_____

_____

_____

_____

_____

Cemetery Plot Information:

Location of document or who to contact: _____

_____

_____

Index

Index

Index

Index

Index

Index

Index

About the Authors

Debby Bitticks, CEO of Delphi Health Products, Inc. is the coauthor of BioBinder™ *Cherished Memories—The Story of My Life* and *Time Efficiency Makeover.* She is also a coauthor of *Chicken Soup for the Soul: Life Lessons for Busy Moms.*

A nationally recognized expert on senior care, Debby has presented and spoken at the National Council on the Aging in Washington D.C. on intergenerational care and has appeared on CBS, NBC, ABC, Fox, *Dr. Phil, CNN Financial News* and other cable shows, as well as giving numerous national radio interviews. Debby has been quoted in articles in *The Wall Street Journal, Los Angeles Times, Chicago Tribune* and *Forbes*, among others.

She has received the Blue Chip Enterprise Award given by the U.S. Chamber of Commerce and Connecticut Mutual Life Insurance Co. Debby is a member of the National Association of Professional Organizers (NAPO) and the National Council on the Aging (NCOA).

For more information on Debby, please visit:
www.biobinders.com
Phone 800 791-8071
Fax 818 784-9437

Lynn Benson, president of Delphi Health Products, Inc. is the coauthor of BioBinder™ *Cherished Memories—The Story of My Life* and *Chicken Soup for the Soul: Life Lessons for Busy Moms.*

Lynn holds a master's degree in social work, with an emphasis on older adult studies and was honored by her university with an "Outstanding Achievement Award." As an executive in the child and elder care industry, Lynn supervised an intergenerational curriculum at numerous centers where she utilized much of her experience to serve the senior community.

As a social worker, while spending countless hours gathering basic information from seniors to complete assessments and provide case management, she realized how

About the Authors

important it is for everyone to have accurate, up-to-date records to provide the most optimal care possible. Lynn's goal with *The Senior Organizer* is to enable people to have immediate access to this life-saving information.

Lynn is a member of the National Association of Professional Organizers (NAPO) and the National Council on the Aging (NCOA).

For more information on Lynn, please visit:
www.biobinder.com
Phone 800 791-8071
Fax 818 784-9437

Dorothy Breininger, America's most trusted professional organizer and CEO of the Center for Organization, devotes her life to teaching people how to design a life you love through organizing your pace (time), face (energy and enthusiasm for life), space (your office or environment) and grace (gratitude and spirit).

Dorothy serves on the board of directors for NAPO (National Association of Professional Organizers), and is a member of the NSGCD (National Study Group on Chronic Disorganization). In addition to being a national speaker and product spokesperson, Dorothy has appeared as an expert on *The Today Show* and *Dr. Phil*, and has been featured in *Forbes, Woman's Day, Fast Company* and *Entrepreneur* magazines.

Among other books, Dorothy is coauthor of *Time Efficiency Makeover* and *Chicken Soup for the Soul: Life Lessons for Busy Moms.* Dorothy's compassionate and successful work with seniors has earned her a commendation by the Los Angeles County Board of Supervisors, and she was awarded the title of "National Small Business Champion of the Year" from the United States Small Business Association.

For more information on Dorothy, please visit:
www.centerfororganization.com or *www.biobinders.com*
Phone: 800-660-GOAL
Fax: 818-718-0711